Alternative Approaches to New Testament Study

Alternative Approaches to New Testament Study

Edited by A. E. Harvey

First published in Great Britain 1985
SPCK
Holy Trinity Church
Marylebone Road
London NW1 4DU

British Library Cataloguing in Publication Data

Alternative approaches to New Testament study.
1. Bible. N.T.—Criticism, interpretation, etc.
I. Harvey, A. E. II. Society for Promoting Christian Knowledge
225.6 BS2361.2

ISBN 0-281-04168-7

Filmset and printed in Great Britain by
Latimer Trend & Company Ltd, Plymouth

Contents

The Contributors

J. DUNCAN M. DERRETT was until recently Professor of Oriental Laws in the University of London

F. GERALD DOWNING is Vice-Principal of the Northern Ordination Course, Manchester

JOHN DRURY is Dean of King's College, Cambridge

MICHAEL GOULDER is Reader in Biblical Studies, University of Birmingham

A. E. HARVEY was formerly Lecturer in Theology at the University of Oxford, and is now Canon of Westminster

LESLIE HOULDEN is Lecturer in New Testament Studies at King's College, London

ALAN MILLAR is Lecturer in Philosophy and Religious Studies, University of Stirling

JOHN RICHES is Lecturer in the Department of Biblical Studies, University of Glasgow

Preface

In modern times the study of the New Testament has been mainly motivated by two concerns: first, to establish a secure connection between the faith of the apostolic age and that of the Church today; secondly, to solve the extraordinarily intricate problems posed by the relationship of the various New Testament writings with each other and to reconstruct the oral and literary processes by which the traditions about Jesus reached their present form. These concerns have set the agenda for New Testament studies for at least a century, and have resulted in the development of a discipline and a method which form the basis of syllabuses in academic institutions and which therefore ensure their own perpetuation. Indeed it could be said that only by being offered such apparently well-tried tools for criticism and reconstruction can the student come to feel that he is acquiring competence in the subject; and that only by continually refining these methods can the teacher feel that he 'knows' more than the student – given that the greater part of all that can be securely 'known' about the New Testament is already available to any attentive reader within the covers of the book itself.

In part this apparently inward-looking approach is due to the peculiar nature of the New Testament as a historical source. Very little information bearing directly on its subject matter is available from other contemporary sources; and even our knowledge of the environment in which it was written is notably thin, and often turns out to be better furnished by the New Testament itself than by any historical sources available outside it. These factors have made it inevitable that critical study should have concentrated on perfecting any means that seemed capable of squeezing further particles of information out of the already familiar text. But such methods are inevitably subject to the law of diminishing returns. Even by ancient standards the New Testament is not a very long book. Most ancient authors who have been the subject of intensive study have written far longer ones. There is a limit to the amount of information which it can be expected to yield, and to the number of patterns in which its various constituent parts can be arranged.

Recent practitioners of the approved methods have been forced to devote their labours to ever more intricate combinations of the available evidence or to ever more abstruse refinements of their predecessors' achievements. It is as if the high ground in the campaign has been occupied long ago. Today's skirmishes concern only residual objectives.

The authors of the essays presented here are all scholars who feel some dissatisfaction with this state of affairs. The available knowledge of the social and religious world in which Jesus and his followers lived has increased substantially in recent years, and forces us to put new questions to the New Testament text; new understandings of method in scientific inquiry force us to review the credentials of hypotheses which have been almost taken for granted for half a century: new disciplines – literary, sociological, anthropological, linguistic – have entered the study of other ancient texts and are clamouring for admission to the apparently closed world of New Testament criticism. Many scholars have in fact begun to take note of these developments and have seen their implications for New Testament studies. But in Britain their impact has been less marked than elsewhere, and those who have sought to bring new life to the subject by these means have often received only a hesitant welcome from the profession, which has moreover become increasingly isolated from the mainstream of theological thinking today.

It is in this sense that each of these essays offers an example of an 'alternative' to the traditional approach. They are also often 'alternative' to each other, in that the authors' positions on many matters are by no means always mutually compatible. But it is our hope that, by assembling this collection of relatively unorthodox studies, a case may be made for actively encouraging new styles of exploration and new contacts with other disciplines. Some of them argue that there may be a richer sense in Scripture than is found in most standard commentaries; others call into question the credibility of the assumptions and hypotheses that are generally brought to bear upon the text. But all share the same concern to open the gates of the citadel to visiting explorers who, even if they occasionally propose unwelcome areas for excavation, may nevertheless contribute to the unearthing of treasures which have lain buried for centuries beneath the weight of conventional but now outmoded fortifications.

October 1984 A. E. HARVEY

1

A House Built on Sand

MICHAEL GOULDER

The Perils of Elasticity

Except when they are debunking the Tübingen School, New Testament scholars do not usually think it necessary to preface their work with philosophical remarks: but all writing contains some philosophical presuppositions, and most current work on the Gospels is vitiated by their neglect. In particular, the work of Sir Karl Popper and of Thomas S. Kuhn in the philosophy of science has been widely influential, if not undisputed.[1] Yet, although directed to science, their work has vital corollaries for other critical scholarship, and not least for what the Germans call *die neutestamentliche Wissenschaft* (New Testament *science*).

Popper wrote *The Logic of Scientific Discovery* in 1934, and an expanded version in 1959; and he wrote numerous papers on allied themes which were published as *Conjectures and Refutations* in 1963. The second title gives the outline of both books in a phrase. What scientists are concerned with is the production of hypotheses or conjectures; and these will be valuable in proportion to the ease with which they can be refuted, or falsified. Thus 'all swans are white' can be refuted by the discovery of a single black swan. A hypothesis which is vague, or elastic, or which claims to account for everything that can happen (like the psychology of C. G. Jung), is unscientific because we cannot refute it; it is not useful because it does not exclude anything. Useful hypotheses will be clear and specific, and if possible elaborate – the word 'baroque' is used as a term of high approbation[2] – because we can then make numerous detailed predictions with their aid. Only one error needs to come to light – one black swan – and we are better off because this hypothesis has now been falsified; but good, corroborated hypotheses will survive for some time, and when they have been refuted, we are often in a position to refine them into new hypotheses, which again will stand for a while. Knowledge advances by conjecture and refutation.

Kuhn wrote *The Structure of Scientific Revolutions* in 1962, with an expanded version in 1970, and he thinks the trouble is more deep-seated. Science is impossible when all we have is an assembly of unrelated facts. It begins when these are put together into a complex of hypotheses, which Kuhn calls a paradigm. This paradigm then becomes a kind of perspective under which all facts are viewed. Paradigms are often brilliant hunches of an early genius, who will hardly get everything right first time. But once a paradigm is accepted it shapes all scientific work: to be a scientist is to accept the paradigm. It is taught in A level textbooks, and all experiments are simply its further working out. 'Normal science', a term used pejoratively by Kuhn, is thus likely to be of limited use in telling us new things about the world. The experiments are suggested by the paradigm, and may do no more than reveal unexpected qualities of phlogiston, or whatever. The history of the subject is told in terms of the paradigm; its professors have made their reputations by assuming and extending it, and will not lightly abandon it. Counter-evidence cannot weary it, for counter-evidence is the spice of life. Occasionally there is the thrill of a hypothesis being found wanting on the fringe of the paradigm; but normally counter-evidence can be accommodated, or will be found erroneous, or can no doubt be explained in time. In this way it is extremely difficult for a shift of paradigm to take place. But anomalies and tensions will build up, and eventually someone will propose an alternative paradigm; and then the Ph.D. students and the young of all ages will suddenly accept it. Shifts of paradigm do not come from professors; they come from young men, and from those on the margin of the subject.

I am not concerned here with the debate between Popper and Kuhn, nor with the difficulties of both positions, which are not negligible; but to stress the obvious peril of elasticity in accommodating anomalies. Both Popper and Kuhn point to this, and it is not without applicability to the New Testament. For the paradigm under which we New Testament scholars work goes back to the beginning of critical scholarship, and was established in the 1830s, at about the time when His Britannic Majesty took the Falkland Islands. It has been developed and refined since, but it is still this which provides the perspective which is taught in the textbooks, and Kümmel's history is told in the light of it.[3] Almost all Ph.D. theses and other gospel studies assume it, and apply it to some new corner. It consists largely of hypothetical lost documents and hypothetical lost bodies of oral tradition. It is almost infinitely elastic, and is virtually unfalsifiable. It is also, as I hope to show in this essay, riddled with contradiction, error, muddle and circular argument. But none of this will suffice to bring it down until an alternative paradigm has been clearly proposed.

I have described a paradigm as a complex of hypotheses; and the standard position, or paradigm, of the Gospels may be said to consist of eight hypotheses.

1 Some parts of all our major Gospel traditions go back to the events and words of Jesus' lifetime.

2 These traditions were treasured and collected in a number of different Christian communities, which both eroded them and amplified them.

3 The first collection to be written down and to survive was made by Mark around AD 70, with further amplifications and erosions of his own.

4 There was a second collection, now lost, which we call Q, preserved in the common non-Marcan matter in Matthew and Luke.

5 Matthew wrote his Gospel about AD 80, combining (conflating) Mark and Q and a third body of tradition to which he alone had access, called M, for the use of a Jewish-Christian church.

6 Luke wrote his Gospel for a more Gentile church, about AD 90, drawing on Mark and Q; he did not know Matthew or M, but had access to a further interesting source, L.

7 John wrote about AD 100, and (on a majority view – a consensus till 1970) had access to traditions also shared by Luke and perhaps Mark.

8 Serious attention should be paid to the Gospel of Thomas, which may sometimes contain earlier forms of synoptic logia and parables.

Paradigms are like the Apostles' Creed. Every reputable scholar subscribes to them in general, just as every Anglican bishop subscribes to the Creed; but doubt is permitted to individual articles, as we have seen in the case of the Bishop of Durham, and the same is true of the paradigm with (for example) the emeritus Professor at Durham, who has been suffered to be doubtful of hypothesis seven, and thinks John used Luke and Mark.[4]

The paradigm I have outlined contained five hypothetical lost bodies of tradition – Q, M, L, the Luke–John tradition, and the Thomas tradition – as well as the even more remote activities of unknown churches, and of Jesus himself: so it is not surprising that it is hard to falsify, and has triumphantly stood the test of a century and a half. The only one of these five lost bodies which is even in principle liable to falsification is Q, and it is worth noting how the issue has been joined, for it is instructive. Q is defined as a body of sayings material and some incidents, beginning from the preaching of John and ending before the passion. At first sight there is virtue in such a definition: for the hypothesis can then apparently be falsified. If there is any significant minor agreement of Matthew and Luke against Mark in the passion story, that will imply that Luke knew Matthew (since Luke wrote later than Matthew, and there is no Q in the passion story). Since Q was originally adopted partly from the erroneous belief that Papias testified to such a document,[5] and partly because it was believed that Luke could not have known Matthew,[6] it might seem that one clear significant minor agreement in the passion story would bring down the whole structure: in which case it will be falsifiable, and so respectable. Of course no amount of minor agreements in the body of the Gospels would be of any use, for the most they could do would be to prove an overlap of Mark and Q: instead of destroying the Q hypothesis, its critics would be congratulated on adding to our knowledge of Q.

Now in fact there is a significant minor agreement in the passion as is widely known:

> Mark 14.65: And some began to spit on him and to blindfold his face and to buffet him, and to say to him, Prophesy!
>
> Matthew 26.67f: Then they spat in his face and buffeted him, and others hit him *saying*, Prophesy to us, Christ, *who is it that smote you*?
>
> Luke 22.63f: And the men holding him mocked him with blows, and blindfolding him they asked *saying*, Prophesy, *who is it that smote you*?

Significant minor agreements are not that easy to come by. Usually it can be found that the changes Luke makes to Mark which agree with Matthew are the same which he makes elsewhere on his own (as in 'ask, saying' here); which is not surprising, as Luke would tend to take over from Matthew his own preferred phrases. Also, there is a common tendency in the copyists to approximate one Gospel to another (especially to Matthew); so that wherever there is a group of manuscripts which lack the agreement, it can be argued that this group has the original text, and the agreement is due to the copyists. But in this case there are no manuscripts to support such a suggestion in Matthew or Luke; and the word 'smote' (*paisas*) is used by Luke here only. So it might seem that we have done it in one: Q (and with it much of the whole paradigm) has collapsed in ruins. There are a number of almost equally damaging agreements elsewhere in the passion narrative, for example five or six details in the account of the burial, or the common use of the unique *epiphōskein*.[7]

The point may seem a simple one to the untutored reader, but I am not writing for the untutored alone. Suppose we scholars were examining a thesis for a doctorate, and the candidate has argued, with much rabbinic learning, that St Paul was a Sadducee. Surely there will come a point at which we shall ask him, 'How then do you account for Paul's own words in Philippians, where he says he was a Pharisee?' We only need the one text to falsify the thesis, just as one black swan falsifies the statement, 'All swans are white'. If the candidate cannot show us a manuscript that has 'Sadducee' (which he cannot), or provide a convincing response to this single point, his thesis must seem to be clearly wrong, and we should fail it. So the question arises, 'Why then do we not fail Q?'

The question why must wait a moment; but the fact is that we certainly do not. What is in fact done is to retain Q, and to adopt a spectrum of suspect arguments for doing so. On the one side there are the hardliners – B. H. Streeter, Josef Schmid, Frans Neirynck and Christopher Tuckett, for example – who have produced and repeated an account of how all the manuscripts of Matthew without exception have been interpolated from Luke.[8] Tuckett concedes that this is not a tidy solution; one may think of stronger adjectives. What is certain is that no one really takes it seriously, for although all the recent editors of the New Testament text are upholders of the paradigm – Kilpatrick, Aland, Metzger, Martini,

Greeven[9] and so far as I know, whatsoever other name is named – none of them prints Streeter's conjecture, nor is it even discussed in Metzger's *Textual Commentary*.[10] Similarly, no commentary on Matthew's Gospel known to me refers to it – Schniewind, Lohmeyer, Bonnard, Schweizer, Gundry.[11] The hard line is limited to explicit defenders of the paradigm.

But there is also, on the other side, a variety of soft lines. For it could be that such agreements were already present in *Ur-Markus*, a prior (lost) edition of Mark, Holtzmann's *Apostolische Quelle*, still championed by W. Schmithals under the label *Grundschrift*.[12] Alternatively, one can suppose a second edition of Mark with the same conveniences, *Deutero-Markus*, as was done by Sanday and Hawkins before the hard line came in, and is represented today by Albert Fuchs.[13] Or there could have been parallel *oral* traditions covering the tender points, as was supposed by Bernhard Weiss, Nils Dahl, W. Kümmel and others.[14] Or there could have been parallel lost written accounts, *Nebenquellen*, as was suggested by Xavier Léon-Dufour and Tim Schramm.[15] But the greatest delight of all would be afforded both to Popper and to Kuhn by M.-E. Boismard's array of *intermediary Gospels*, where the lost editions are multiplied with a contempt for William of Occam which is a wonder to behold.[16] Finally, of course, there is the softest line of all: to *concede* that Luke knew Matthew, but to maintain that he also knew Q as well. This is the position of Morgenthaler and Gundry.[17]

With an increasing embarrassment over the weakness of the hard line, the soft line is becoming more popular; and even hardliners like Neirynck and Tuckett hedge their bets, pointing out that if forced to concede the minor agreements battle they will still not have lost the Q war. What then is wrong with it? Its trouble is, in Popper's terms, that it has ceased to be falsifiable. As long as we had a firm definition – Q had no passion story – it looked as if this was a hypothesis excluding certain phenomena – Luke did not know Matthew, so there could be no significant minor agreements in the passion story. But once any of the soft lines is adopted, nothing is excluded: *we can never know that we are wrong*. Hedley Sparks said of Boismard, 'the more complicated the theories . . . become, the more questionable and less obviously compelling they necessarily are.'[18] But it is worse than that. We not only condemn ourselves to uncertainty, we put ourselves beyond correction. In Kuhn's terms, it is far more menacing. The paradigm of the 1830s has become 'normal science'. Anomalies are resolved by the invention of a cloud of possible but unevidenced epicycles. This is the standard recourse of the imperilled orthodoxy. No one knows what the defence is. Most teachers of New Testament in universities do not believe any of the options on offer, and continue to use the paradigm simply because they do not know what else to do. As Joseph Fitzmyer puts it, the synoptic problem 'has thus far failed to find a fully satisfying solution'[19] we just continue to use the paradigm because it is *brauchbar* – or in English, because it has been used for 150 years. Nothing, in other words, will shift it but a revolution.

The Matthaean Vocabulary Fallacy

Our anxiety at finding ourselves thus exposed is much increased by two further factors. One is the extent of the structure which we have built upon the questionable foundation of the Q hypothesis alone. For it is not only books on the Christology of Q, or the community behind its traditions, which are at stake. All views of the Gospels of Matthew and Luke depend upon the paradigm; and so, often, do studies of Mark, where his wording is compared to Q versions, and so on. Any attempt to renew the quest of the historical Jesus is involved: C. H. Dodd's *The Founder of Christianity*,[20] for example, takes Q as its earliest evidence. Theologies of the New Testament, attempts to trace the development of christological belief, and all such endeavours have to take a position on the paradigm, and the position that is invariably taken is its acceptance. The other disturbing factor is the volume of self-contradiction, circular argument and error which is involved in its application. I shall now give a few instances of what I mean, and of how the paradigm is vitiated at every step.

The basic decisions which a scholar makes in applying the paradigm are the separation of the editorial activities of the evangelists from the 'tradition', the source they are working on. Let us consider first the way in which the work of Matthew is distinguished from his sources. Three methods are used. First, one may take as 'Matthaean' the changes Matthew makes to Mark (assuming Marcan priority) – verbal, doctrinal and general stylistic changes. Secondly, one may attribute to Matthew link-phrases and formulas. Thirdly, one may reckon that where phrases come with an undefined frequency in Matthew's Gospel, even if they are never used in the redaction of Mark, they are likely to be due to the evangelist. I have no criticism of any of these methods. When we see Matthew writing *oligopistos, oligopistia* into his version of Mark at 8.26, 16.8 and 17.20, it is obvious that we should attribute the same word to Matt.R at 14.31.[21] It is plain that connecting phrases like 'And it came to pass when Jesus had completed all these words . . . ', with its fivefold use in Matthew, is Matthew's own writing. Or again, a phrase not in a connecting section, like 'there shall be weeping and gnashing of teeth', occurring six times in Matthew, is by the evangelist himself.

The trouble arises when we look at the QC material (the words in Q which are common to Luke and Matthew). For all these expressions just cited, which are among the most striking Matthaeanisms there are, also occur in single instances in Luke, in QC words. Matthew 6.30 'will he not much more clothe you, *oligopistoi*?' is paralleled in Luke 12.28, 'how much more [will he clothe you], *oligopistoi*!'; so *oligopistoi* has to be credited here to Q. Thus Q, like Matthew, hesitated to speak of the disciples as without faith, as Mark did, and respectfully lamented their 'little faith' – although *oligopistos* is a word not attested before Matthew. Similarly Luke 13.28, 'There will be weeping and gnashing of teeth when they see Abraham . . . ' is parallel to Matthew 8.12, 'There will be weeping and gnashing of teeth'; so here again there is a Matthaean phrase in Q. Thus Q shares Matthew's enthusiasm for the pangs of hell. Even the ultra-Matthaean, 'And it came to pass when Jesus had completed (*etelesen*) all these words (*logous*)' at Matthew 7.28, has an embarrassing parallel at Luke 7.1, 'When he had fulfilled (*eplērōsen*) all his words (*rhēmata*)', where *pleroun* and *rhēma* are more Lucan words, and both contexts end with Jesus entering Capernaum. As Luke, *ex hypothesi*, did not know Matthew, Heinz Schürmann has to suppose that Matthew was taking over a Q formula here also.

In this way Schürmann can escape with his Q intact; but he does not notice what has happened to his critical method *en route*. For the purpose of the method was to enable us to distinguish what was Matthaean redaction from what was in the source, here Q. But in the event it has turned out that all the phrases which we had established as being characteristic of Matthew were also used by Q! Nor can we plead that a single use in Q is different from a regular use in Matthew: there are 1800 words in QC and 18,000 words in Matthew. In repeated and significant instances, Matthew's style and Q's are indistinguishable – that is, Schürmann cannot distinguish them.

If I had just chosen three special examples to suit my case, this might not matter. But in fact it is a very general issue, and involves the whole method in self-contradiction. I take as an instance the first full paragraph in Q, the Baptist's preaching, partly because it is the first, and partly because eighty-three out of eighty-nine words are identical, QC.[22] John begins, '*gennēmata echidnōn*, you generation of vipers, who warned you to flee from the wrath to come?' Now *gennēmata echidnōn* occurs again twice only in the Gospel tradition, at Matthew 12.34, and at Matthew 23.33 ('You snakes, you generation of vipers'). But Matthew also makes a speciality of offensive vocatives followed by rhetorical questions. 12.34 again, 'You generation of vipers, how can you speak good, being evil?'; 23.17, 'You fools and blind, which is greater, the gold or the temple?'; 23.19, 'You blind, which is greater, the gift or the altar?'; 23.33 again, 'You snakes, you generation of vipers, how shall you escape the judgement of hell?' Such a combination does not seem to occur in Mark or L. So Q and Matthew share not only a penchant for the phrase *gennēmata echidnōn* – and indeed for comparing those they disapprove of to snakes more generally – but also for the offensive-vocative/rhetorical-question form. (All the other passages just cited are 'M'; and it is open to the reader to substitute 'Matthew's source' for 'Matthew'. But then distinguishing the styles of M and Matthew is also an embarrassing difficulty.)

In the next verse we meet the phrase *poiein karpon*, to make fruit, and this recurs in 3.10. It is in fact a common phrase in Matthew's Gospel, occurring ten times (but only six times in Luke and not at all in Mark), and is introduced by Matthew himself at 21.43R as well as at 12.33 and 13.26M – indeed the whole of 3.10 comes again at Matthew 7.19, 'every tree that makes not good fruit is cut down and cast into the fire.' As it is not in Luke at this point in Q, it seems to be Matthew's own addition. For not only is 'make fruit' rather Matthaean; so are the combinations 'cut down and cast' and 'cast into the fire'. *Ekkoptein-kai-ballein* comes twice in redactions of Mark (5.30, 18.8), and sinners *are cast into the* furnace of *fire* at 13.42M and 13.50M. Furthermore, much of the final verse of the

Baptist's address looks strongly Matthaean, 'he will gather his corn into the garner (*synaxei ton siton autou eis tēn apothēkēn*), but the chaff he will burn (*katakausei*)'. Not only is *synagein* a favourite word of Matthew's (occurring twenty-four times in Matthew, five times in Mark, six times in Luke; 26.57R), but the whole vocabulary recurs at the end of the Tares (Matthew 13.30 alone): 'Bind (the tares) in bundles to burn (*katakausai*) them, but gather the corn into my garner (*ton siton synagagete eis tēn apothēkēn mou*)'.

In this way we may see that of the eighty-nine words in John's sermon, eighteen form part of Matthew's vocabulary elsewhere – *gennēmata echidnōn, poiein karpon* (× 2), *ekkoptein kai ballein eis pyr, katakaiein/synagein ton siton eis tēn apothēkēn.* It would be easy to add individual words which Matthew is fond of, like *oun* (fifty-seven times in Matthew, five times in Mark, thirty-one times in Luke) or *dendron* (twelve times in Matthew, once in Mark, seven times in Luke): but in a way the phrases are best left on their own for impressiveness. Of course it might be that Matthew enjoyed the Q phrases and copied them in elsewhere. But then the only phrase we find in the passage that is also in Mark is the colourless 'I say to you that'. There is no Q passage of Matthew that has anything approaching twenty per cent of its words/phrases from Mark, still less seven words together as in 3.12, or an entire sentence like 3.10.

On the paradigm we might have hoped that Q would preserve for us some authentic, individual tones of the Baptist; but the fact is, as I have illustrated, that the Baptist not only speaks with the same tones and phrases as Jesus, but with the same tones and phrases as the Matthaean Jesus. Some simple-hearted followers of Occam might be beguiled by this into reducing the number of hypotheses, since we now have one too many. Since Q's vocabulary and Matthew's seem to be the same, and since sophisticated defenders of the paradigm will allow that Q is post AD 70, and so in the same decade as Matthew, and also shares most of Matthew's theology, it looks as if either Q or Matthew could go.[23] Either Matthew wrote Q, or Q wrote Matthew. This solution is however open to two obvious and fatal flaws, as is pointed out by Gerhard Sellin.[24] First, it is 'definitely too simple', and secondly, it contradicts the paradigm. Nevertheless, the evidence I have adduced, and which I can parallel for every considerable section of Q, shows this part of the standard position to be self-contradictory and unworkable. All arguments of the form, 'This is Matthaean, so the Lucan version of a QD phrase will be earlier', are invalid.[25] Since Matthew's style is to such an extent the same as Q's, it is just as likely that Matthaeanisms are Qisms. We thus have a major fallacy on our hands, which I shall call the Matthaean Vocabulary Fallacy.

The Lucan Priority Fallacy

I move on now to a second error of method in the paradigm, which is its circularity, or assuming what it is supposed to prove. When a textbook on the synoptic problem considers the academic question of whether Luke knew Matthew – say Streeter's *The Four Gospels* – one of the main reasons given is that sometimes Luke, sometimes Matthew, has the earlier form of a Q logion. This would apparently conclude the matter. However, when we ask how the earlier Lucan forms are identified, we find a number of arguments used, many of them weak and reversible; but by far the most common is that the style of the Matthaean form is Matthew's own style. Thus, which is earlier, Matthew's 'he will assign his portion with the hypocrites', or Luke's 'with the faithless'? Luke is earlier, because Matthew likes *hypocrites*. Which is earlier, Matthew's 'you are like graves', or Luke's 'tombs'? Luke, for Matthew is fond of *taphos*, a grave. There are hundreds of examples of this.

Now this argument is fallacious twice over. First it is circular. How do we know that *hypocrites* is Matthaean? Because, of course, Matthew has it thirteen times, Mark once, Luke three times. But then that might also imply that Luke *dis*liked calling people hypocrites. How then do we know that Matthew did not edit the earlier form of the tradition, using *hypocrites*, and Luke change it to *apistoi*, in contrast with the *pistos* (faithful) servant at the beginning of the parable? We don't. Of course paradigmers are perfectly aware that this is a theoretical possibility; but in practice it is never mentioned because it would violate the paradigm. Thus we have a perfect circle. Luke knew Q, not Matthew, because sometimes (as here) the Lucan form of a Q logion is prior. We can tell the prior Lucan form by Matthew's redaction in the Matthaean form. This cannot be due to Luke's changing Matthaean redaction, because Luke knew Q, not Matthew. Of course the circle would not matter if sometimes Lucan priority in Q logia could be established by other methods; but these other methods do not seem to be forthcoming. Two views can be, and very frequently are, available on every other argument; and it is arguments of the above type which are much the commonest on offer. On their own, therefore, they must constitute a second fallacy, the Lucan Priority Fallacy. The argument is also defective because of the Matthaean Vocabulary Fallacy which I have already discussed, so that it is doubly valueless. In the instance of the servant parable there is an abundance of Matthaean phrasing, like 'Amen I say to you that . . . ', 'that servant', 'his lord', 'faithful and wise', 'the day and the hour'.

Now when there are Matthaean words in the Matthew versions, there are, naturally, words in the Lucan version which fall on a spectrum of Lucan-ness. *Apistos* comes only once elsewhere in Luke, once in Acts, so the Lucan priority argument looks plausible; but *mnēmeia* (tombs) Luke uses quite often (seven times). As Luke has the largest vocabulary of the Evangelists by a long way, it is not surprising that he uses his words less often than Matthew, with his rather stereotyped phrasing; and I will comment on the Hapax Legomenon Fallacy below. But the point is that the spectrum has two extremities. Sometimes Luke uses his word rarely, and then the Luke-knew-Matthew view must supply an explanation (as I have with the link with *pistos* above). But sometimes also Luke has a very Lucan word, and this causes an embarrassing dilemma for the paradigm, through an *embarras de richesses* of explanations. For on the normal view one or the other of the Gospels has preserved Q for us – once we allow that they may *both* have changed Q, the reconstruction of Q is going to become *sehr spekulativ*; and that will be the end of it. So we will expect to find Matthew changing a phrase here and Luke one there, but not both at the same time. On my hypothesis just mentioned, however, we should expect a lot of Matthaean phrases in Matthew's compositions, and when Luke does not like them he will sometimes substitute Lucan phrases. That is exactly what we do find.

The address of the Lord's Prayer is an obvious example. Much of the wording of the Prayer in Matthew and Luke is identical, and with the unique word *epiousios* (for the coming day) in common, they must be directly related, or else depend on a common Greek source, that is to say Q. Matthew begins, 'Our Father who art in heaven', and this is a favourite phrase of Matthew's: no commentator would dare to suggest that this is other than Matthew's own change, or he would sabotage his whole method. For some reason critics are not so quick to observe the Lucan nature of Luke's plain *pater*, Father. But on two further occasions in the passion story Luke has the word on Jesus' lips – 'Father, forgive them . . . ' (with some textual doubt), 'Father, into thy hands . . . ' – and Luke's Prodigal Son says it three times (15.12, 18, 21). Thus it stands on its own, plain vocative *pater* (comma), six times in L or the Lucan form of Q; *and Luke also substitutes it himself* for Mark's *abba ho patēr* at 22.42. If this were not enough, we may notice that (where Matthew writes 'my Father' and so on), Luke writes other plain vocatives, 'brother' (6.42R), 'child' (× 3), 'friend'. A paradigmer like Siegfried Schulz does not even notice this, but takes Luke's *pater* to be a translation of Jesus' *abba*,[26] though it may be noticed that *abba* is used three times in the New Testament, and each time with a translation, and it is never *pater* but always *ho patēr* (Romans 8.15; Galatians 4.6; Mark 14.36).

The Lucan/Pre-Lucan Style Fallacy

For a second example of circular argument I take the celebrated 'refined method' of Heinz Schürmann.[27] I preface my comments with a word of admiration for Schürmann. There is no finer commentator on Luke. He has an encyclopaedic reading behind him, an unerring eye for significant detail, and an acute spiritual perception for situations and motives. But his refined method is a sad instance of circular arguing, of caution masquerading as method, the more damaging because his influence has been so wide, and every paradigmer is infected with it.

Schürmann is trying to be as careful as possible. How can he be sure of what words to count as Lucan? He limits the number to those where Luke is making alterations to Mark; Luke is taken to be making alterations to Q; and the second half of Acts. He is refining the older method, where sheer numbers of uses were included; for they might come in good number simply because they were in Luke's sources. But then refinement of method turns out to be as perilous as the refinement of food. For clearly if Luke has supplied almost half of all the words he has in Marcan passages, and up to half of all the words in the Q passages, we might expect him similarly to have written up to half the words in the L passages. So Schürmann is in a predicament over phrases in the L passages, that is to say most of the Gospel: he will not, for caution, attribute them to Luke's redaction, and yet up to half of them may be just this, and he cannot tell which.

The practical result – since decisions have to be taken – is to assign many things to Luke's source (L, the *Sondergut*); but this involves repeated circular argument. 'Simon, Simon,' says Jesus, 'Satan has desired to have you . . . ' the repeated name recalls other repetitions in Luke–Acts: 'Martha, Martha . . . ', 'Saul, Saul . . . ' Nor do we find such in other Gospels: but then 'Martha, Martha' is in an L passage, and should therefore not be counted as Luke's editing, and 'Saul, Saul' is in the first half of Acts and may be traditional. One might object that Luke changes Mark's 'Teacher' in the storm-stilling to 'Master, master'; but this is not a name. So 'Simon, Simon' goes down as part of the evidence for a special-Lucan (L) source in the passion story. Or again at Luke 22.17 Jesus received, *dexamenos*, a cup. *Dechesthai* is in fact a common Lucan word, but Schürmann observantly notices that Jesus doesn't receive it *from* anyone – he just takes it, and this makes it a rarity. In fact it comes only twice elsewhere in the New Testament in this sense, in Luke 16, where the unjust steward says twice, 'Take (*dexai*) your bill'. This might suggest to anyone else that we have the hand of Luke in both passages; but to Schürmann Luke 16 is an L passage, and so *dexamenos* is further evidence of his special Lucan source behind the Last Supper.

Even a word like *plousios* (rich), which comes three times in Matthew, twice in Mark, eleven times in Luke, and which Luke actually writes into Mark at 18.23, is dismissed by Schürmann from being Luke's own. It never comes in Acts, he says, and eight of the eleven uses in Luke are in L, with a further two following Mark; while 18.23 is drawn in from the Marcan uses close by. But then Acts is not about rich people, and Schürmann has no means of knowing whether the uses in L were in the source or not. His method is simply circular. It merely assigns all doubtful words to Luke's sources, and they then become evidence for Luke's use of sources![28]

The Hapax Legomenon Fallacy

So far we have mainly considered the problem arising from the positive techniques – those which are supposed to isolate the style of the evangelist. But what about isolating what was *not* the evangelist's style? For this is required (as we have just seen with

Schürmann) if we are to find what has been contributed by the source. Just as multiple use of an expression within one Gospel, especially in editorial passages, is a sign of the evangelist's activity, so is the converse taken to be true. If an expression is used once only in a Gospel – unless in an editorial passage – that is an indication that it comes from a source; and in any passage one can discriminate the evangelist's source from his over-writing by the presence of *hapax legomena*, or once-used expressions. Thus we do not go far in any discussion before finding some scholar like Georg Strecker stating, 'Unmatthaean are a few hapaxlegomena . . . ';[29] and we find the same argument on every page of Schulz's study, *Q* – in fact every paradigmer requires this string to his elbow.

It is rare to see the argument behind this technique actually set out. It can hardly be, 'People do not use an expression only once in a writing without taking it over from elsewhere'; for self-evidently we all use, when writing on our own, a grade of frequency of expressions, from once up to many times. We could formulate the argument more gently: 'If an expression occurs once in a work using sources, it is more likely to come from the sources than from their editor.' Even this does not sound overwhelmingly convincing, because it may depend on the size and regularity of a man's vocabulary. We are at once warned to be wary, for example, by the fact that Luke, who has written two books in the New Testament, may have a word once only in one book, and quite often in the other. *Keleuein*, to command, for instance, is used seven times in Matthew, never in Mark, and once in Luke, so there is a Matthaean, non-Lucan word – or it would be if it did not come seventeen times in Acts. Or more widely, Luke and Acts are similar in length, but Luke (on the paradigm) contains much source material, for a source is supposed to underlie every pericope in the Gospel, while Acts is taken to be almost source-free in the we-passages and speeches, that is to say half the book: so on the *hapax* argument there should be a lot more *hapaxes* in Luke than in Acts. But in fact there are 971 *hapaxes* in Luke and 943 in Acts; with 19400 words in Luke and 18400 in Acts, the figures are virtually level.

We can, however, be more specific than this, and as this argument is so central to the discussion it is worth while putting it to a proper test. This is not difficult to do, for we have a considerable body of material in Luke which is widely agreed to be taken over from Mark and partially rewritten. This is the so-called pure Marcan tradition, in the three blocks: Luke 4.31—6.19 (less 5.4–9, the catch of fish); 8.4—9.50; and 18.15—21.4 (less 19.1–27, Zacchaeus and the pounds). Together, this material comprises 4643 words, which is quite long enough for statistical comparisons. We can then divide the words into two, those which are taken over from Mark, and those which Luke has written in himself. The division is almost in halves: 2362 words are in common with Mark, on my computation, and 2281 are not. So for once we have a falsifiable theory: clearly we are to expect the source material to contain more *hapaxes* than the redaction. We can now count up the *hapaxes* – and for this purpose the *hapaxes* have to be words that occur once only in Luke (not Luke–Acts) – or we shall not be able to compare the figures in other Gospels. There are 173 *hapaxes* in the whole: seventy-one of them fall in the Marcan words and 102 in the non-Marcan words. So the exact reverse of what is assumed by the technique turns out to be true. There are not only more hapaxes introduced by Luke than there are in his source, Mark, but many more, forty-four per cent more. So the whole argument is based on a fourth fallacy, the *Hapax* Fallacy.

But if this is the case, it may be replied, how would anything ever be allowed to count as pre-Lucan? This will indeed be a difficulty for those who work from concordances alone; but not otherwise. I have already noted the abusive vocative/rhetorical question sequence as being foreign to Luke, and other locutions dear to Matthew. I will suggest in a moment the double animal imagery as the stamp of a mind other than Luke's. Luke knows a few Jewish phrases like 'the nations of the world', but he almost always gets Jewish technicalities wrong, and they would, if accurate, suggest a pre-Lucan source. So would anything that implied a pre AD 85 situation, like the tower that fell in Siloam, or the Galilaeans whose blood Pilate mingled with their sacrifices. Clusters of *hapaxes* would also be a cause of suspicion – Luke could not have written 2 Peter. There are many ways in which a source gives itself away; but isolating a single word and looking it up in a concordance is not one of them.

An Alternative Paradigm

Kuhn says that a profession will not desert the old paradigm till a new one is proposed; and I can hear my friends and colleagues sighing with groans that cannot be uttered. 'Ah, wretched man that

I am', they say, 'Who will deliver us from the body of this death?' No man dare say that he will replace a false paradigm with a true one, but I can propose a new one for the old, and that I will now do.

Of the eight hypotheses which constituted the old position, seven are false. The only true one is Marcan priority.[30] The eight hypotheses which I am proposing are as follows.

1 Some parts of Mark go back to the events and words of Jesus' lifetime. It is possible but doubtful that there are reliable traditions in the non-Marcan sections of the other Gospels.

2 The Marcan traditions were collected and treasured by the Jerusalem community under Peter, James and John, which amplified and eroded them.

3 They were written down by Mark about AD 70, with further amplifications and erosions of his own.

4 There was no lost sayings-source common to Luke and Matthew. Q is a total error.

5 Matthew wrote his Gospel about AD 80, as an expansion of Mark for a Jewish-Christian church. He was a competent scribe, a fine parabolist, and an inspired poet; and the Q and M matter in his Gospel is almost entirely his own creation.

6 Luke wrote his Gospel about AD 90 for a more Gentile church, combining Mark and Matthew. He re-wrote Matthew's birth narratives with the aid of the Old Testament, and he added new material of his own, largely parables, where his genius lay. The new material can almost always be understood as a Lucan development of matter in Matthew. There was hardly any L.

7 John wrote about AD 100, for an Asian church with a different foundation than the synoptic churches and with acute doctrinal problems. He drew on all three Synoptists, but especially Matthew, and developed them freely. He did have other traditions, of dubious reliability.

8 No serious attention should be given to Thomas, which is a gnosticizing version of the Gospels, especially Luke.

Although so much of this essay has been given to demolition, or deconstruction (to use the jargon), I do not wish the reader to feel that the methods used by so many learned and astute scholars before me are to be despised as valueless. I do think that these methods have been used with insufficient criticism, but I do not at all take them to be utterly wrong. I cannot, in a few pages, support my proposed paradigm in detail, but I can add a few comments on the way in which standard methods can be revised and improved.

A basic fault with the present methods is that they are commonly confined to words, or combinations of words. These are usually few in number, and conclusions are often drawn from the presence of three or four uses, simply because that is taken to be all the evidence there is. We need to look round for broader categories. I give six instances, three from Matthew and three from Luke.

In the editorial sections, Matthew often includes words in couples that are virtual clichés, like Pharisees-and-Sadducees: 'he went round the towns-and-villages, teaching . . . -and-preaching . . . healing every-sickness-and-every-disease'. Of course everyone uses cliché-pairs like this, but the point is, they are a sufficiently common feature to be worth counting – and the above sentence, with three in it, suggests that Matthew himself is keen on them. If I am right about Q and M, then we should find quite a lot of cliché-pairs in both sections – and that is precisely what we do find: heaven-and-earth, the-law-and-the-prophets, sackcloth-and-ashes, Sodom-and-Gomorrah – they come in far larger numbers in Q and M alike than they do in Mark and L, and they come in the Matthaean form of a good number of Q sayings, but not the Lucan: jot-and-tittle, moth-and-rust, break-through-and-steal, and so on. Such a feature would not prove my hypothesis, but it would corroborate it; and, as Popper says of scientific theories, that is all we can hope to do.

At first sight the occurrence of a Matthaean phrase, like 'weeping and gnashing of teeth' in a single Q-passage in Luke, looks like evidence that Luke knew Matthew; but, as we have seen, the paradigmer can always reply, 'Q used the phrase, and Matthew took it up – just as Mark has "your Father in heaven" once, and Matthew takes that up.' This response is not implausible with doctrinally loaded phrases, but it would be much less likely that Matthew would take up an odd quirk of style that had no doctrinal edge. There may be a number of such phrases, but one that comes to mind is Matthew's fondness for following *anthrōpos* with a noun. He has a merchant man at 13.45M, a householder man at 13.52M, 20.1M,

21.33R, and a king man at 18.23M and 22.2M; but he also has a glutton and drunkard man at 11.19, where Luke has the same combination, here and here alone, at Luke 7.34Q. It is surely more plausible to see Luke as carrying over a Matthaean locution here, than to see Matthew taking up a phrase of Q's.

Imagery is more revealing than language, because the type of images we use shows a basic cast of mind, and one does not change an image as easily as one does a word. Much of Jesus' teaching must have been expressed in images – wine and patches, houses and strong men, the whole and the sick, and so on – and since different collectors of his sayings would be unlikely to cut out whole groups of images (as they might cut out whole groups of teachings), we should expect to find any widespread group of his images turning up in several collections (perhaps all). However, on my hypothesis, Matthew has been responsible for both the M and the Q material himself, so they will contain *his* images: and we should then expect to find them in M and Q but perhaps not in Mark or L. Now there is a particularly attractive and memorable group of logia which make use of *two animal images* in a single saying; they are images in the sense that the traditional character of the animal is made to symbolize some aspect of Jesus' ministry – not just part of the scenery, like the bulls and fatlings of Matthew 22.4. These might even serve as a test case between the two paradigms. Anyhow, there are ten of them, and here they are:

Do not give dogs what is holy, and cast not your pearls before swine.
Or if he asks for fish, will he give him a serpent?
Who come to you in sheep's clothing, but inwardly are ravening wolves.
Foxes have holes, and birds of the air have nests.
Behold, I send you out as sheep in the midst of wolves; so be wise as serpents, and innocent as doves.
You blind guides, straining out a gnat and swallowing a camel!
You snakes, you brood of vipers!
. . . gathered your children together as a hen gathers her chicks under her wings.
He will separate them, as a shepherd separates the sheep from the goats.

All ten come in Matthew! There are none in Mark or L, but there are three which have parallels in Luke (Q), the fish/serpent, the foxes/birds and the sheep/wolves in the form of lambs/wolves.[31] This seems to me in some ways a decisive argument, because the combination of pairs of animals in this symbolizing way is the work of a single mind. If it were Jesus' mind, it really would be extraordinary if neither Mark nor L preserved a single instance. If one wished to extend the argument to pairs of natural images, there are figs and grapes, thorns and thistles, and moth and rust; and these all come in Matthew too.

With Luke, similarly, the area of attention needs to be broadened from the language to the mode more generally: I close with three instances. We find in Luke's Gospel alone a sequence of proportions of *one in ten*. The woman had ten drachmas and lost one; there were ten lepers and one returned to give thanks; the nobleman has ten servants and one of them is faithless; he gives them a *mna* apiece, and one of them makes ten, and is made governor of ten cities. Of the two debtors, one owes five hundred pence and one fifty. This looks like a habit of mind again, especially as the structure of the pounds requires three servants as in Matthew, and Luke actually refers to the third as 'the other' (19.20).

A common expression of Luke's is *anastas*, getting up; and this again, by virtue of its frequent insertion by Luke in Mark, suggests that Luke was himself a man of active, 'get-up-and-go' temperament. We notice the same trait in a number of other passages in Luke:

Mary arose and went *with haste* into the hill country.
They went *with haste* and found Mary and Joseph.
That when he comes and knocks, they may open to him *at once*.
Go out *quickly* into the streets and lanes of the town.
Take your bill, and sit down *quickly*, and write fifty.
Zacchaeus, *make haste* and come down.
So he *made haste* and came down.

There are instances, of course, of prompt action in Mark and Matthew, but alacrity seems to be a special feature of Luke. He knows, too, the virtue on occasion of the opposite:

Which of you . . . does not first sit down and count the cost?
Or what king . . . will not sit down first and take counsel?

In Luke alone we find instances of what we may call the *guillotine question*: that is, where the interlocutor is manoeuvred into placing his own head on the block. 'Simon', says Jesus menacingly, 'I have something to say to you'; and tells him the parable of the two debtors. 'So which of them', he ends, 'will love him the more?' The cornered Pharisee mumbles the correct reply, 'I suppose he to whom he forgave the more'; and down comes the knife, 'You have judged right.' So again with the tempting lawyer in Luke 10: Jesus does not cite *him* the Scripture, as he does in Mark and Matthew. Luke wants his head on the block, so he has Jesus ask, 'What is written in the Law? How do you read?'. The man replies with Deuteronomy and Leviticus, and down comes the guillotine again: 'You have answered right: do this and you will live'. But this time the evangelist has not finished. The man objects, 'And who is my neighbour?', and Jesus counters with the Good Samaritan. So the parable already has the doomed aristo in his tumbril, and with the final question, 'Which of these three do you think was neighbour?', he submits, and Luke has his head in the basket. Twice in an afternoon!

A paradigm is not like a single hypothesis which can be refuted at a blow. It is a complex of hypotheses, and the Gospel paradigm that we have grown up with is hallowed by over a century's use by all the most famous critics. It is more a perspective, a cast of mind, a presupposition of a lifetime's work for many of us; and I do not labour under the illusion that I shall overthrow it in an evening.[32] It will not be abandoned with the publication of this essay, nor yet with the two-volume, eight-hundred-page work which I hope to publish under the title *Luke, Mark and Matthew*. I am asking for a shift of paradigm; and Kuhn is surely right to say that such shifts do not take place without strong resistance.

In such a matter it is important to avoid excessive claims. I have not set out an alternative paradigm as yet. The major part, a verse-by-verse accounting for Luke's Gospel on the assumption of his use of Matthew, and with minimal assumption of Sondergut traditions, has not yet seen the light. I have in the press an outline account of Luke's ordering of Matthew, the biggest of the stumbling-blocks.[33] As for my earlier *Midrash and Lection in Matthew*, I do not think my colleagues to be stiff-necked who have not been persuaded by its theses; for it is marred by inexperience, and a frequent lack of awareness of their perspective. In the long run, there will be some who will not be persuaded however great the evidence; and of them it is written, 'Neither will they believe though one should rise from the dead'. But, despite Kuhn, I retain an optimistic confidence in the integrity of my profession as a whole. If they are not persuaded, it will be either because I have explained the position badly, or because I am wrong.

However, this essay is not concerned to establish, but only to adumbrate, an alternative paradigm. Its central object is not constructive at all. I cannot tell you that I have built my house upon the rock, only that, like the Lucan builder, I have dug and deepened and laid a foundation. But I can, and do tell my colleagues that the method they have been using is bankrupt. It is vitiated by self-contradictions, circular arguments, dilemmas and fallacies; and this has been concealed from them by the historical development of their paradigm, which has deprived them of any means of knowing when they are wrong. What I hope to have shown is that their tool is broken. Their house is built on sand.

NOTES

1 Neither is mentioned, for example, in Humphrey Palmer's *The Logic of Gospel Criticism*, London and New York 1968. For a discussion of Popper and Kuhn, cf. I. Lakatos and A. Musgrave, *Criticism and the Growth of Knowledge*, Cambridge 1970.

2 Cf. John Rodwell, 'Myth and Truth in Scientific Enquiry', in *Incarnation and Myth*, edited by M. D. Goulder (London 1979), p. 67.

3 W. G. Kümmel, *Das Neue Testament. Geschichte der Erforschung seiner Probleme*, Freiburg 1958, ET London 1973.

4 C. K. Barrett, *The Gospel according to St John*, 2nd edn London 1978.

5 Papias, Bishop of Hierapolis *c.* AD 130, wrote that 'Matthew arranged the sayings (*ta logia*) in the Hebrew language' (Eus. H. E. 3.39). F. Schleiermacher suggested in 1832 that this Matthew was the apostle whose collection came to the evangelist (Kümmel, *Introduction to the New Testament*, 14th edn, ET 1966, p. 38), and from the late 1830s the *logia* were taken to be the non-Marcan source common to Matthew and Luke. It was referred to as the Logia till the 1890s, and in German is still often called the *Logienquelle*, although it has been recognized for many decades that it contains more than logia, and that Papias was speaking of Matthew's Gospel. Thus Q was based on a mistake from the start.

6 There were exceptions to this opinion: H. J. Holtzmann, *Lehrbuch der Historisch-Kritischen Einleitung in das Neue Testament*, 3rd edn (Leipzig 1892, pp. 356–8, thought Luke knew Matthew as well as the Logia.

7 These (and other) significant minor agreements are discussed in my 'On Putting Q to the Test', and 'Mark 16. 1–8 and Parallels' in *NTS* 24 (1978), pp. 218–40.

8 Streeter, *The Four Gospels* (London 1924), pp. 325–9; Schmid, *Matthäus und Lukas* (Freiburg 1930), pp. 157–9; Neirynck, *The Minor Agreements of Matthew and Luke against Mark* (Leuven 1974), p. 179; Tuckett, 'On the Relationship between Matthew and Luke', *NTS* 30 (1984), pp. 136ff. Neirynck merely catalogues the opinions of others here, but is himself the foremost defender of the general hard line. Tuckett is specifically replying to my essays in note 7.

9 G. D. Kilpatrick, *Hē Kainē Diathēkē*, 2nd edn, London 1958; K. Aland, *Synopsis Quattuor Evangeliorum*, 4th edn, Würtemberg 1967; K. Aland, M. Black, C. M. Martini, B. M. Metzger, A. Wikgren, *Novum Testamentum Graece*, Nestle-Aland, 26th edn = UBS 3rd edn, Stuttgart 1979; H. Greeven, *Synopse der drei ersten Evangelien*, Huck, 13th edn, Tübingen 1981.

10 B. M. Metzger, *A Textual Commentary on the Greek New Testament* (UBS 3rd edn, 1971), p. 65.

11 J. Schniewind, *Das Evangelium nach Matthäus, NTD*, Göttingen, 11th edn, 1964; E. Lohmeyer–W. Schmauch, *Das Evangelium des Matthäus*, KEK 3rd edn, Göttingen 1962; P. Bonnard, *L'Évangile selon Saint Matthieu*, Neuchâtel 1963; E. Schweizer, *The Good News according to Matthew*, London 1975; R. H. Gundry, *Matthew*, Grand Rapids 1982.

12 *Das Evangelium nach Markus*, Gütersloh 1979.

13 W. Sanday, *Studies in the Synoptic Problem* (Oxford 1911), pp. 3–26; J. C. Hawkins, *Horae Synopticae* (2nd edn, Oxford 1909), p. 212; A. Fuchs, *Sprachliche Untersuchungen zu Matthäus und Lukas* (AB 49, Rome 1971).

14 B. Weiss, 'Die Erzählungsstücke des apostolischen Matthäus', *Jahrbücher für Deutsche Theologie* 10 (1865), pp. 319–76, especially p. 365; N. A. Dahl, 'Die Passionsgeschichte bei Matthäus', *NTS* (1955), pp. 17–32; W. Kümmel, *Introduction* (n. 5), p. 50.

15 X. Léon-Dufour, *Studia Biblica et Orientalia* II (AB 11, Rome 1959), pp. 116–28; T. Schramm, *Der Markusstoff bei Lukas*, SNTS 14, Cambridge 1971.

16 M.-E. Boismard and P. Benoit, *Synopse des Quatre Évangiles en Français*, vol. ii *Commentaire*, Paris 1972.

17 R. Morgenthaler, *Statistische Synopse* (Zürich–Stuttgart 1971), pp. 301ff; R. H. Gundry, *Matthew* (n. 11), pp. 4f.

18 H. F. D. Sparks, review of Boismard (n. 16), *JTS* (1974), p. 486.

19 *The Gospel according to Luke* I–IX (Anchor, Garden City 1981), p. 65.

20 C. H. Dodd, *The Founder of Christianity*, London 1973.

21 Matt.R, Lk.R = Matthew's and Luke's own contribution as 'redactor' overwriting their sources.

22 Matt. 3.1–6, the introduction to John's ministry, is often reckoned today as a Mark-Q overlap (A. Polag, *Fragmenta Q*, Neukirchen-Vluyn 1979, p.28); but the Baptist's Sermon in Matthew 3.7 – 10, 12 par. is universally agreed to be Q-material by defenders of the paradigm.

23 Earlier defenders of the paradigm put Q about AD 50; but it is now realized that it contains a number of references to the fall of the Temple (Matthew 23.35f par., 23.37f par.) and the delay of the Parousia (24.48 par.). This enables some to distinguish two, or even three, stages of Q!

24 'Lukas als Gleichniserzähler: Die Erzählung vom barmherzigen Samariter', *ZNW* 65 (1974), p. 175.

25 QD: words in Q which are different in Matthew and Luke. QC: words in Q which are the same in (common to) Matthew and Luke.

26 *Q. Die Spruchquelle der Evangelisten* (Zürich 1972), p. 85.

27 Schürmann discusses questions of method in his review of F. Rehkopf's work, 'Protolukanische Eigentümlichkeiten?' reprinted in *Traditionsgeschichtliche Untersuchungen*, Düsseldorf 1968: the phrase occurs on page 209.

28 *Jesu Abschiedsrede* (Münster 1957), p. 101; *Der Paschamahlbericht* (Münster 1953), pp. 23f; *Das Lukasevangelium*, I (Freiburg–Basel–Vienna 1969), p. 337, n. 88.

29 *Der Weg der Gerechtigkeit* (FRLANT 82, Göttingen 1966), p. 150.

30 It is ironic that the only national community to be at all seriously troubled about the paradigm is that in America, where William Farmer has led a small movement to challenge it on the basis that Marcan priority is an error (cf. Fitzmyer's comment above, n. 19). Although Farmer's arguments cannot be maintained (cf. C. M. Tuckett, *The Revival of the Griesbach Hypothesis*, *SNTS* 44, Cambridge 1983), American scholars have not been wrong in sensing that something was amiss with critical orthodoxy.

31 In Matthew Jesus is sending out the apostles ('the twelve') as sheep; in Luke he is sending out the seventy-two, whom Matthew refers to as 'these little ones' (10.42) – so he pictures them as 'lambs'.

32 A version of this essay was read to the British section of the Society of New Testament Studies in Edinburgh, on 21 September 1984.

33 'The Order of a Crank', in C. M. Tuckett, ed., *Synoptic Studies: The Ampleforth Conferences of 1982 and 1983*, *JSNT*, Sheffield 1984; *Midrash and Lection in Matthew*, London 1974.

2

Mark 1.1–15: An Interpretation

JOHN DRURY

I

In 1835 D. F. Strauss published his *Life of Jesus Critically Examined* and lost his tutorial post in the Evangelical seminary at Tübingen. The bite of the book's title is in the words 'critically examined', for it was not really a life of Jesus at all but a critical examination of the Gospel texts. It had an immediate effect on Strauss's career and a long-term corrosive effect on the understanding of the Gospels.

The critical method of Strauss is both formidable and simple. First, he shows that the narratives as they stand are incredible and impossible. Second, he shows that modern naturalistic interpretations of them are worse than useless. The book largely consists of the relentless and consistent application of this destructive pincer-movement. In terms of the passage before us, it is incredible and impossible that the sky split open and that God spoke in Greek. To say that this was really a thunderstorm is worse than useless because it implies that the text, with all its theism and theology, is based on a mistake, and at the same time it empties it of any religious value.

After this demolition, Strauss offered his reconstruction. The narratives are myths, constructions of the Christian imagination which has been formed and informed by Old Testament Scripture. In the Old Testament the sky is a great stretched tent which can, therefore, be split. The words which God speaks are a quotation of Psalm 2.7 and Isaiah 42.1. The job of the myth is the great Christian job of displaying the divine authentication of Jesus persuasively: that is, in terms of what was agreed to be authenticating in matters of divinity, the holy Scriptures.

Strauss took one more step. It was to have occupied a whole subsequent book but is in fact crammed into a postscript. Myths are ideal and poetic kinds of narrative. Strauss shared the belief of many intellectuals of his day that they were the philosophy of the people. They therefore provide an escape route from the ruined historical edifice of conventional Christianity into the universal realm of idea and spirit. There Christianity survives as dogma.

Poignantly, this last step which Strauss thought so redemptive of the situation turned out to be his false move. In the view of his great teacher, F. C. Baur, he had done well up to this point but here denied the intrinsically historical nature of Christianity and removed it from historical study. Baur was an historian who opposed the etherealizing or evaporating of Christianity into ideas alone. Rather, Christianity was matter for the modern historian: a developing interaction of ideas and events, of intellectual and social-political history. Both were integral.

Unfortunately, few scholars reacted as judiciously as Baur. Frightened by Strauss they flung the machine of criticism into reverse and have spent the subsequent 150 years largely in an attempt, to which English scholarship has contributed massively, to reconstruct the naturalistic historical base of Christianity. They have striven industriously, and with meagre results, against what was true in Strauss's analysis: that the Gospel texts are ineluctably constructions of the Christian imagination. They have striven against it in that, while acknowledging its truth, they have tried to pierce through the theologized texts *down* to the historical actuality. This is the matching and opposite mistake to Strauss's. He tried to get through the texts *up* to the dogmatic and abstract import. Both went through the text on the way to other things.

In categorizing both these reactions to the discovery of myth in the New Testament as mistakes, I am betraying my debt to structuralist literary criticism. Structuralism is the way of reading which refuses the notion that texts are windows through which the eye might pass and then espy the heaven of ideas or of history *wie es eigentlich gewesen*. It is a deliberately blinkered method which tries to read only text and to follow it as if it were music. I have found it to have the functional recommendation of getting me to see things in the text which I have not seen before. But I come to structuralism as one who studied history and admires Baur. That means that I agree with Strauss up to, and short of, that last dematerializing and ahistoricizing step. I see the Gospel texts as imaginative narratives to which naturalistic interpretation is not apt. Strauss's identifying of the pervasive influence of the Old Testament upon them gives his work abiding practical value; and it sets my structuralist reading in history. The New Testament generally, and the Gospels particularly, are part of an historical process: the early Christians' primary struggle to commandeer the whole sacred and scriptural past as the authentication of their religion, of their Christ. That is not how we would authenticate Christianity now, but it was then. As what you commandeer always in some degree commandeers you, so the Old Testament is a code in the structure of these Christian narratives. Structural reading can thus be checked against an historical correlate: the early Christian strategy of taking over the historic tradition of Judaism. Roland Barthes says, in a footnote to his essay 'Introduction to the Structural Analysis of Narrative' that 'there does, of course, exist an "art" of the storyteller which is the ability to generate narratives (messages) from the structure (the code)'.[1] This is a qualification of Barthes' doctrine of the unimportance of authors; but a very important one, creating a margin on which the historian can work. The narrative which we will now look at is precisely a message (gospel) generated from the code whose structure is the Old Testament. It has to be generated for Christianity to survive its critical and delicate immediately postnatal years. It has to consume the Old Testament, generating its message from its code.

II

In the diagram the all-important narrative line runs from top to bottom. It is indicated by the arrowed lines going downwards in the left-hand 'time' section. It would be worth while to tip the diagram through ninety degrees so that that line runs along the bottom of the tilted sheet from left to right – the usual way in which we, as opposed to Chinese or Jewish readers possibly, imagine its progression. Tip it back again and to the left of the arrowed lines you can see bits of the Old Testament code which structure the narrative. They are not in the order of the Old Testament books, chapters and verses. This does not mean that Old Testament order does not matter at all. On the contrary, we shall see that it does very much – and not least in the strategy of reversing it or running it backwards. It does suggest that this fragmentation and reversal might be the effect of another but related code working on the story, the gospel of Jesus which is put in the third column next to the text. It connects and relates with the Old Testament column *via* the John Baptist column that comes

TIME

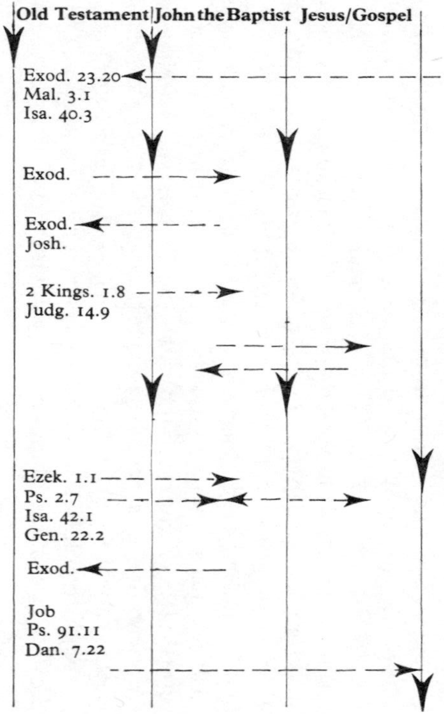

Old Testament | John the Baptist | Jesus/Gospel

Exod. 23.20
Mal. 3.1
Isa. 40.3

Exod.

Exod.
Josh.

2 Kings. 1.8
Judg. 14.9

Ezek. 1.1
Ps. 2.7
Isa. 42.1
Gen. 22.2

Exod.

Job
Ps. 91.11
Dan. 7.22

MARK 1

THE BEGINNING of the gospel of Jesus Christ,
the Son of God.
2 As it is written in Isaiah the prophet,
"Behold, I send my messenger before thy face,
who shall prepare thy way;
3 the voice of one crying in the wilderness:
Prepare the way of the Lord,
make his paths straight—"
4 John the baptizer appeared in the wilderness,
preaching a baptism of repentance for the forgiveness of sins. 5 And there went out to him all the
country of Judea, and all the people of Jerusalem;
and they were baptized by him in the river Jordan,
confessing their sins. 6 Now John was clothed with
camel's hair, and had a leather girdle around his
waist, and ate locusts and wild honey. 7 And he
preached, saying, "After me comes he who is migh-
tier than I, the thong of whose sandals I am not
worthy to stoop down and untie. 8 I have baptized
you with water; but he will baptize you with the
Holy Spirit."
9 In those days Jesus came from Nazareth of
Galilee and was baptized by John in the Jordan.
10 And when he came up out of the water, immediately he saw the heavens opened and the Spirit
descending upon him like a dove; 11 and a voice
came from heaven, "Thou art my beloved Son;
with thee I am well pleased."
12 The Spirit immediately drove him out into
the wilderness. 13 And he was in the wilderness
forty days, tempted by Satan; and he was with the
wild beasts; and the angels ministered to him.
14 Now after John was arrested, Jesus came into
Galilee, preaching the gospel of God, 15 and saying,
"The time is fulfilled, and the kingdom of God is at
hand; repent, and believe in the gospel."

PLACE

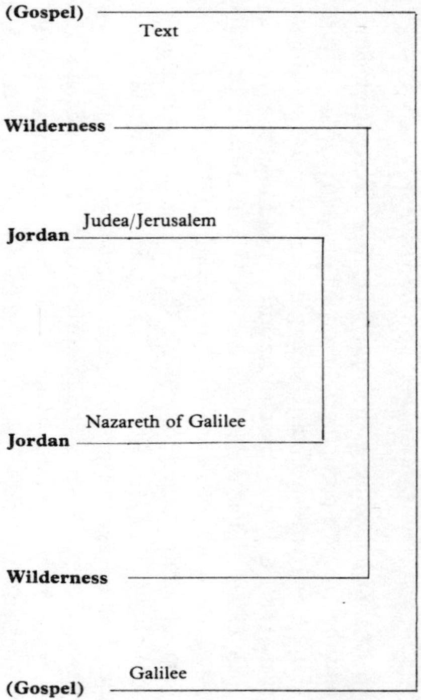

(Gospel)
Text

Wilderness

Judea/Jerusalem
Jordan

Nazareth of Galilee
Jordan

Wilderness

Galilee
(Gospel)

between the two of them and is the actual and overt storyline until the crux of verses 9–11, after which the third column is the storyline. The other thing to notice about the Old Testament code-string is that, far from going its own sweet way, it feeds and binds into the other two strands or columns and they into it. The broken arrows which go to and fro across the strands or columns (I will call them 'strands' from now on) show this happening.

The arrows matter in another way too. Barthes uses two major categories in his essay. They are functions and indices. They work like the warp and the weft in weaving.

Functions 'go off', in Barthes' phrase, along the narrative line or horizontally. They are hinges in the narrative. They inaugurate or conclude an uncertainty – or both. They have correlates. 'The essence of a function is, so to speak, the seed which it sows in the narrative' (p. 89). Barthes instances the first mention of 'parrot' in Flaubert's *Un Coeur Simple*: germinal, because in the end the parrot will appear to the dying housemaid, the 'simple soul', divinely transfigured. Of the numerous instances of such functions in Mark 1.1–15 – such as 'voice', 'baptism', 'spirit' – we could choose right now as an illustration 'wilderness'. The Scripture of Isaiah speaks of wilderness (strand one), John Baptist appears in it and all Jerusalem and Judea join him there (strand two), Jesus (strand three) is driven into it to be tempted for forty days.

Indices, on the other hand, work vertically rather than horizontally. Barthes says they are 'data regarding . . . identity, notations of atmosphere'.[2] They give depth or height. Just as the ratification of a function was always further on in the story, so the ratification of an index is always higher up or further down. In verses ten and eleven of our text we have an index with a vivid monumentality beyond the dreams of the Parisian critic. The horizontal narrative vibrates up and down with seismic intensity. Jesus came up (Greek, *anabainōn*) out of the water, the spirit comes down (Greek, *katabainon*) on him. God's climactic 'thou art my beloved Son' is an indication of identity from above of imperial clarity. Where could one find a better instance of Barthes' index? Or, come to that, of his function, since both happen here simultaneously in an explosive crux. Jesus's sonship proclaimed or 'indicated' *in baptism* sows a seed in the narrative and functionally points to a later ratification or ratifications. We know, historically, that for Mark as for Paul baptism was a death-ritual of adoption into the sonship of

God which is the Christian's inheritance. 'Do you not know (Paul appeals to common knowledge) that all of us who have been baptized into Christ Jesus were baptized into his death?' (Romans 6.3). Mark shares this theology or myth of the baptism ritual. At Mark 10.39 Jesus tells James and John 'The cup that I drink you will drink; and with the baptism with which I am baptized, you will be baptized.' What is the cup? We learn at Mark 14.36 in Gethsemane that it is the agony of death. So also, by close association in Mark 10.39, is baptism. The series of interconnected functions, which at the outset of the book was marked by the index of God's voice at Jesus' baptism declaring him his Son, clinches at Mark 15.39 where Jesus dies and the centurion declares 'truly this man was the Son of God'. Both baptism and death are marked by tearings: of the sky in one, of the temple veil in the other. They connect.

Are we seeing patterns in the fire, clouds that are dragonish? For the structuralist, no: since there is no noise but only music in literature, and what is noted is notable. It is a dogma that I am disposed to accept. But again I remember Baur's strictures on Strauss and *his* positivism of dogma and want historical checking before I assent.

Early Christian historiography was, as noticed earlier, an attempt to capture the traditional religious power base and authenticating authority of Scripture. Paul's letters show him retrospectively fitting the entire sacred history – Adam, Abraham, Isaac, Moses – into Christianity as its grand Proto-evangelium. The writer of the Epistle to the Hebrews saw the holy past in the same way, as a preparation, as a series of functions waiting for the conclusive index of Christ. In Mark's narrative, short on doctrinal reflection and rich in occurrences, the holy past is implicit in his currently narrated series of events. Let us see how.

Just now, in considering the major theme of baptism, we saw it as a seminal function, going off and ratified at later stages in the narrative. Baptism belongs in the middle or 'John Baptist' of the three strands in the diagram. What we have seen so far, from the evidence in Paul and Mark of the Christian theology of baptism, is the relation of it to the Jesus strand which is marked fore and aft by the gospel which is the Christian gospel. In this context it is absolutely no coincidence that Mark's Jesus begins where Mark's Christians began as Christians, with baptism. Beginnings of text and of Christian life synchronize. If we now want to see the reinterpretation of the past at work we will need to see the John/Baptism strand in its relation to the Old Testament strand.

As we just noticed, Mark 1.1–15 begins and ends with gospel. It is announced at 1.1. Jesus comes out actually preaching it at 1.14, 15. What happens between is thus the gospel's germination, and to this the Old Testament is fundamental: unmistakably so in verses two and three which quote it overtly. 'Who is speaking thus?' as Barthes asks of another story.[3] The answer must be one that would have pleased him. No one is speaking. This is text, 'as it is written'. The text in question is a seed-packet of functions, foretelling a preparer in the wilderness. Immediately the preparer appears in *the* wilderness. What is *the* wilderness for a Bible reader? It is the wilderness of the exodus where Israel was for forty years before entering the land by crossing the Jordan. There, then, is John Baptist preaching a baptism of repentance. Then an astonishing thing happens: too astonishing for Vincent Taylor (*The Gospel According to St Mark, ad loc.*) who says lamely that it must be something of an exaggeration.[4] 'And there went out to him all the country of Judea, and all the people of Jerusalem; and they were baptized by him in the river Jordan, confessing their sins.' '*All* the country of Judea and *all* the people of Jerusalem?' we ask, questioning whether it be seriously meant. It is: Mark is running the nation's history backwards. Once they had all come out of the wilderness over the Jordan and settled in Judea and the city of Jerusalem. Now city and land stand empty as they go back to the threshold of their inheritance, the Jordan; and not just to it but into it, to be baptized, and to be baptized by the forerunner who is dressed as Elijah (2 Kings 1.8), and whose wildness and belonging to the world before culture are evident in his dress and his diet, which includes the wild honey eaten by the wild Samson (Judges 14.9). It is a vast backtracking. As we follow it as readers we are told what baptism is. There is no immediate need to consult historical encyclopaedias. The Bible is the place to look it up. It is Jordan baptism, a going through water to get the promise. The next and inevitable event in the same place is the archetypal Christian baptism, the baptism of Jesus. It is, as it were, laid over the previous baptism and fulfils it, for when Jesus is baptized and comes up from baptism, the story is momentarily halted by the descent of the indices of God's validation: dove, spirit and voice.

But only momentarily. At verse twelve the story is moving strongly, impelled by nothing less than the spirit which drives Jesus into the wilderness. Still the movement is backwards. All the people came to John and were baptized in the Jordan. Mark, who is an emphatic and deliberate writer, does not emphasize that they came to the wilderness. It is implied only. Here with Jesus it is explicit. He is driven into the wilderness which is, in the great national and sacred story, the other side of the Jordan from the land and city. The note of forty days means that this cannot be mistaken or ignored, since Israel was forty years in the wilderness, tempting and tempted, before Jordan was reached. So Jesus is driven backward into the primal history. There he is with wild beasts, whereas the people had previously met only a wild and beast-like man. There he is with supernatural beings, angels, whereas the people had previously only met one agent of the supernatural: John the messenger (Greek *angelos* at Mark 1.2). Only after this ultimate ordeal of the primitive, for which the rolling back of history was necessary, can the Christian story proper begin with Jesus preaching the gospel of God. By then it has consumed the Old Testament history into itself and can go forward with time fulfilled.

Looked at another way, as ritual rather than literature, we have seen something very like a rite of passage. Here the right-hand side of the diagram helps. The goal of the narrative is set up at the outset and reached at the end. It is gospel or message. It is proclaimed at the beginning and very deliberately and artlessly *as* beginning: 'the beginning of the gospel of Jesus Christ'. Gospel happens at the end when, John put aside, Jesus comes into Galilee preaching the gospel of God. Between those two points is the crossing over, vividly evident as such in the palindromic symmetry of the diagram. It is a great threshold: 'great' in the sense of containing other thresholds. The wilderness was the betwixt-and-between land of the exodus from Egypt to the promised land. Jordan was the threshold between the wilderness itself and the promised land: a thinner and finer threshold. But there is a yet thinner and finer one, the margin of the Jordan and the land on either side of it. And it is here, when Jesus comes up out of the water, that the revelatory catastrophe takes place: the authentication of Jesus by spirit and divine voice. The same spirit propels Jesus back into the wilderness, and only after that primal and supernatural ordeal does he come into Galilee a new and empowered man who preaches the gospel announced at the outset and is in Galilee (not just Nazareth of Galilee), which is for Mark the holy land.

The rite of passage is the birth of Christianity, going back into the womb of sacred history and passing its ordeals in order to be born into present and future. The narrative which tells it is precisely what it says it is, 'the beginning of the gospel of Jesus Christ, the Son of God'. It is the happening or 'going off' of its title.

III

The sort of structural analysis which I have done is looked at askance by New Testament scholars who still approach the Gospels to distil from them the actual and historical events of Jesus's life. It looks as if there is nothing in it for them, to whom it will appear as a flight from history and actuality. Anyone who has been trained historically will have some sympathy for them.[5] But it was the negative achievement of Strauss to show that the gospel texts do not lend themselves to the sort of reconstruction that they want to do, and a century and a half of attempts to do it nevertheless have failed to come up with assured enough results to annihilate Strauss. The historically trained critic who wants to remain such has therefore to shift his ground and the field of his inquiry to the texts themselves. Hence the appropriateness of structural analysis. But hence also the need to make historical sense of what such an analysis brings to light. I will end by attempting that.

First, as has been already said twice, the text of Mark 1.1–15 shows us an early Christian writer christianizing the Old Testament tradition: by quoting it as christological, by rerunning – in a striking instance, by reversing – its formative events such as exodus, Jordan and the entry into the Promised Land. This recapitulating strategy is not singular to Mark. All the major New Testament writers do it. Paul in his letters makes Christ the second Adam, the antitype of Moses, the fulfilment of the promise to Abraham, the rock-cum-fountain of the exodus. There is the Moses typology in John's Gospel. Matthew's infancy narratives are an unmistakable instance of the same procedure. So are Luke's. The Revelation of John is only comprehensible along these lines. Time fulfilled in the Christian gospel of Christ is the overriding principle of all their work.

It is no coincidence that for so many of them the exodus is the favourite material for Christian retreatment. How Judaism came to be is the template for how Christianity came to be, and its authentication. This is more than formal. It gives the religious depth inherent in a rite of passage. The dangerous crossings-over which people go through in so many ways, and have to go through to live, were vivid to the early Christians: corporately in the emergence of their faith, individually in conversion and baptism. Baptism gives us a precise purchase on this text. Perhaps chief among the things which the critics have not noticed in it is that Mark thought baptism the point for his narrative to begin. Why did he? Because he was writing as a Christian for Christians and that is the point at which their Christian lives began. The text about Christ which is also a mosaic of Old Testament text is further a text about Christianity in the first century. It is there that it refers historically to something outside text – though, as we have seen, this is a life textually nourished and formed. This is not a new insight. Strauss had it. R. H. Lightfoot's *Gospel Message of St Mark* uses it convincingly to show the binding of the fate of Jesus into the fate of his disciples. The narrative primacy of baptism, the Christian rite of passage, the death sacrament enabling new life, achieved this for him and his readers with disconcerting power and would have alerted them to the way the narrative had to go on to the outcome which they knew. The later Gospels of Matthew and Luke modify Mark's beginning by their curiosity about Jesus' birth.

If we have not got exactly what happened to Jesus, but have got a reordering and repossession of the past around a momentous crossing over, we still have something of historical and religious value. Of historical value because it lets us right into the world of early Christianity and gives us a taste of its historical and historiographical energy. Of religious value because, if it does not give us historical naturalism – and it certainly does not, as Strauss insisted – it gives us something which (if we are religious at all) is arguably better: the realism which Dostoyevsky claimed when he professed: 'I am called a psychologist. It is not true. I am only a realist in the highest sense of the word, that is to say, I depict the depths of the human soul.' Those depths are most palpable in the haunting pattern of the rite of passage. It suggests very strongly indeed the presence of the same pattern in Jesus' actual biography: that he suffered or initiated a crossing of boundaries in a real rather than a ritual or literary manner. Whether such a momentous (if now not recoverable) crossing ended in oblivion or in some new and practicable way of living depended on those who came after him and on whether they could authenticate and ratify it. They did, and from a text such as this we can recover how they did it.

NOTES

1 In *Image – Music – Text*, ed. and tr. Stephen Heath (Hill and Wang, New York 1977), p. 80.

2 Ibid, p. 92.

3 'The Death of the Author'; *Image – Music – Text*, p. 142.

4 Compare this passage from W. B. Yeats 'The Trembling of the Veil', in *Autobiographies* (1955), p. 154:

> Passing another day by the new Law Courts, I grew suddenly oppressed by the great weight of stone, and thought, 'There are miles and miles of stone and brick all round me,' and presently added, 'If John the Baptist or his like were to come again and had his mind set upon it, he could make all these people go out into some wilderness leaving their buildings empty.'

The moral is clear. It takes an imaginative person to take this passage literally.

5 On p. 8 of the third edition of his *The Birth of the New Testament* (London 1981) C. F. D. Moule says of structuralism that 'it scarcely concerns the processes by which the New Testament came to birth . . . It is clear, at any rate, that in so far as structuralism plays into the hands of treating the New Testament documents on a purely literary level, without regard to historical questions, it tends to eliminate a vital factor in the study of Christian origins.' The tendency which Moule deplores has been resisted in this essay, in which structuralism has been found to illuminate 'the processes by which the New Testament came to birth' when used in relation to the history of the emergence of Christianity, particularly its authentication of itself by its historiography. This is not, of course, the same thing as the quest for the historical Jesus. But the history of how various people thought about history, to which this essay is a tiny contribution, is an indispensable part of historical inquiry. It can, after all, have dramatic results in their behaviour. The patterns on the 'purely literary level' may become patterns of historical action, ways people physically go. Josephus, in his *Jewish Antiquities* XX. 97, gives an example of particular interest to this study:

> During the period when Fadus was procurator of Judea, a certain impostor named Theudas persuaded the majority of the masses to

> take up their possessions and to follow him to the Jordan river. He stated that he was a prophet and that at his command the river would be parted and would provide them an easy passage.

This attempt to re-enact the exodus was abortive – literarily and historically. It is referred to at Acts 5.36, but shorn of its all-important typology.

3

Conceptual Change in the Synoptic Tradition

JOHN RICHES & ALAN MILLAR

I

Considered from one point of view, a text is a series of inscriptions or marks on a surface. From another, it is a series of sayings. The interpreter of a text wants to know what it says. Putting the matter in this way highlights the important distinction between, on the one hand, linguistic entities, sentences and other expressions, and, on the other hand, the senses possessed by these expressions on particular occasions of use. The interpreter seeks to bridge the gulf between the knowledge of what inscriptions a text contains and the knowledge of what is being said through these inscriptions by the author of the text. To recognize this truism is already to appreciate that from an epistemological point of view the *senses* possessed by the expressions occurring in a text are not *hard data* – they have to be inferred. A principal theme of this paper is that determining the sense of the expressions in a text or spoken discourse involves the identification of a network of beliefs which are systematically related to one another, which are anchored, however loosely, in experience and which sometimes also have implications for human practice.[1] Where biblical texts are concerned it would be a mistake to suppose that there is some purely linguistic level at which we could determine what the texts say without consideration in detail of the content of the theological concepts and beliefs which they articulate. If we fail to grasp these concepts and beliefs we fail to understand the texts. It is all too easy to pay lip-service to this insight for want of an adequate appreciation of the extent to which concepts and beliefs are systematically related to one another and to experience and action. In this first section we shall say something in fairly general terms about the nature of these relationships. Our remarks are of a sort more commonly found in works on the philosophy of language. We find them to be suggestive for the practical business of interpretation.

Knowing what would be said by uttering a declarative sentence in some context is a matter of knowing what belief would be expressed by the sentence in that context. In the sense intended here 'belief' is synonymous with 'proposition' and refers to something which can be held to be true. The term 'belief' is, of course, also used for the state of holding a proposition to be true. One who believes that God cares for his creatures has a belief-state whose content is the proposition (belief-content) that God cares for his creatures. Certainly there is more to understanding a text than uncovering the propositions which are expressed by its declarative sentences. Understanding, in its broadest sense, would encompass the motives and purposes which the text's authors or editors had in writing or compiling it in just the way they did. But inquiry into such matters must go hand in hand with the identification of the underlying pattern of thought. Without that, neither motives nor purposes could be discerned or made intelligible.

Ignoring certain complications, we may take it then that, in the central sense intended here, to understand an utterance (inscription) of a sentence is to know what proposition the sentence uttered (inscribed) expresses. There are two components in such knowledge. To understand an utterance of *S*, where *S* means that *p*, we must not only grasp the proposition that *p*. Also we must know that *S* means that *p*. One could meet the first condition without meeting the second. A person who does not understand English could grasp the proposition that God cares for his creatures while being unaware of the fact that the English sentence 'God cares for his creatures' expresses that proposition. We shall consider below, very briefly, how propositions are attached to sentences. First we must consider how propositions relate to one another and to experience and action.

To grasp a proposition is to know what would have to be the case if it were true. Essentially the same point can be expressed by saying that to comprehend a proposition is to comprehend its inferential power – to know what can be inferred from it and also how it can be combined with other propositions to yield conclusions which could not have been drawn from each separately. The example already used will serve to illustrate this claim. From

1 God cares for his creatures

we can infer

2 God wants to promote the well-being of his creatures.

The validity of this inference reflects the concept of caring. *Anyone* who cares for something must (logically) want to promote its well-being. If now we combine (2) with

3 If God wants to do something he does do it

we may infer

4 God does act in ways which promote the well-being of his creatures.

The validity of the inference from (2) and (3) to (4) turns on the concept of conditionality – the concept expressed in English by 'If —— then'. A person who grasps (1) is acquainted with the inferential powers of (1) to the extent of being able to draw out these and other inferences. Such a person is able to locate (1) within a network or web of propositions related logically to it in ways which exhibit its constituent concepts.

By itself the notion of inferential power does not suffice to explain what it is to grasp a proposition. Propositions must come down to earth and this they do via their links with experience and action. Some have as constituents concepts which apply to observable things. Anyone who grasps the concept of a garage must know what garages look like as well as knowing that a garage is a place for storing or repairing motor vehicles. To know that something is a garage is to know, among other things, that it will yield visual experiences falling within a certain range. But even propositions which do not contain concepts applicable to observable things can have experiential implications. If this were not so, then high-level scientific theories would not be testable. It is characteristic of religious thinking within a theistic framework to regard the world as being what it is because God has made it and to hold therefore that the world is as it should be expected to be if made by God. Precisely what one expects the world to be like if made by God will depend on the inferences which one draws from fundamental theological propositions and these, as we have already remarked, will exhibit one's understanding of these propositions. Differences in what people infer will reflect differences in their understanding and these differences will be most telling when they pertain to the sorts of things which people see and feel. Theologies which stress the radical sinfulness of humankind yield very different expectations about what human beings are like from those which retain in substance the idea that man is in the image of God.

Another way in which theological propositions come down to earth is through their practical implications. Differences in theological understanding yield different conceptions of how people ought to be and of what they ought to do. Current controversies about liberation theology are at least in part due to differences over the practical implications to be drawn from propositions about God. These differences reflect divergent understandings of theology. The idea that people could agree on basic doctrine but radically diverge on practical principles does not hold water.

Our remarks thus far have been designed to elucidate what it is to grasp a proposition. A major task for the theory of meaning is to explain how it is that sentences express the propositions they do. While there is no generally agreed account of this matter it is plausible to suppose that sentences express what they do because of conventions which govern the use of their constituent expressions. For example, among speakers of English the following is a convention:

> For any *x* and *y*, where ‘x’ and ‘y’ range over English referring expressions (such as proper names or singular descriptions), if one accepts ⌜*x* cares for *y*⌝ then one accepts ⌜*x* wants to promote the well-being of *y*⌝.

(‘⌜*x* cares for *y*⌝’ should be read as ‘the result of concatenating *x* with “cares for” and *y* in the manner shown’.)[2] It cannot be too strongly emphasized that conventions of the sort described deal with *words* in particular languages. Earlier, when speaking of the inferential powers of propositions, we observed that the inference from (1) to (2) reflected the *concept* of caring. That concept was identified by means of English expressions but, of course, could be grasped by people who do not understand English. Now we are speaking of the English *expression* ‘cares for’ and suggesting that the reason why it expresses the concept that it does lies in conventions such as that described above.

The distinction between expressions and concepts is of considerable importance for understanding the relation between the conventional links which bind together the expressions of a particular language and the logical (non-conventional) links which bind together the concepts and propositions attached to these expressions. That is a philosophical topic which need not be pursued here.[3] Our interest in the distinction has to do with the light it casts on the relation between the inscriptions in a text and conjectures about what they mean. Clearly, ascriptions of meaning to a text ought to be consistent with the conventions governing the expressions it contains. In the case of ancient texts in dead languages we have, by and large, no access to the relevant conventions except through the texts themselves. What we must do is assign meanings which square with such conventions as the text makes it plausible to suppose actually obtained. That is to say, we must seek to identify a set of logically interrelated propositions which matches the conventional relationships for which the texts in question and any other relevant sources provide evidence. This general idea and our previous remarks on how propositions relate to one another and reach down to experience and action give substance to the following suggestions about method in biblical interpretation.

First, we ought to countenance the possibility that the network of expressions which is relevant to fixing the sense of a given expression may be much wider than we at first think. For example, we are sometimes told that the concept which Paul expresses by the Greek term *dikaiosunē* (righteousness) is juridical rather than ethical. This claim would seem to ignore the way in which, in Romans, Paul contrasts the wickedness of both Jews and Gentiles, which he spells out in explicitly ethical terms, and the righteousness of God (Romans 3. 1–8). It also fails to take into account the possibility that there are logical connections between being righteous, as Paul understands that notion, and conforming to the ethical injunctions of Romans 12—15 – connections which might well be mediated by the Pauline concepts of faith and of the gifts of grace. We have nothing to lose and everything to gain from casting the net wide in our search for textual evidence for the sense of *dikaiosunē*. If we do not, we could fail to appreciate how the beliefs which lie behind the relevant texts ramify and ultimately bear upon the problems of life. Later we shall make similar observations on the concept of the Kingdom of God in the synoptic tradition. The situation there is complicated by the many strata which underlie the texts. Even so, we should not allow a quite proper concern to identify the provenances of various sayings to blind us to possible interconnections between sayings and to possible implications of sayings which the texts do not make explicit.

Secondly, we must be sensitive to the fact that one and the same expression may have a number of different senses. What a person means by the English term 'democracy' will depend upon the conventional uniformities governing the person's use of the term. The network of conventional links which reflects the use of the term by a Marxist of Stalinist inclinations will be rather different from those of a New Right conservative. Nevertheless there will be a degree of overlap between the concepts of democracy which they determine. *All* concepts of democracy pertain to rule by the people but what in detail that amounts to will depend upon the wider networks in which the concepts figure. The analogies between the concepts which make each of them concepts of *democracy* do not testify to fundamental affinities of thought. Although this point is uncontroversial when put in these terms, it is easily ignored. This happens, for example, when the key terms of a text are assumed to have the sense they bear in some source which may have influenced its author. Yet it is obvious on reflection that an author or editor who takes over some linguistic expression or the core of some concept need not be borrowing uncritically. He or she might be concerned to change more or less radically the ways in which the expression or concept has hitherto been understood.

One of the shortcomings of the History of Religions school was its tendency to 'explain' texts primarily in terms of their historical roots. Paul's doctrine of the End was to be explained out of (*erklären aus*) Jewish apocalyptic ideas of resurrection, election, judgement, and the like, which in turn were supposed to have their origin in Iranian, Zoroastrian doctrines and earlier Jewish ideas.[4] Other aspects of Paul's thought might be traced back to his Pharisaic heritage or to the Greek mysteries. A classic example of this kind of approach is given by Pfleiderer in his account of Pauline theology which he compares to two streams, one Pharisaic, one Hellenistic, running together into one bed yet remaining discrete.[5] This whole tendency to identify two strands in Paul's thought has a long history which starts with Lüdemann's attempt to isolate two anthropologies in Paul's thought, one Jewish, the other dualist.

We would not wish to dispute the claim that there may well be elements in Paul's thought which are not well integrated, or are perhaps even inconsistent. Indeed the theoretical perspective outlined above makes it quite reasonable to suppose that someone may make substantial conceptual changes without necessarily thinking through all the implications of such changes. A writer like Paul might change many of the conceptual connections of a particular concept while retaining some which were at odds with the new content he gives to the concept. On the other hand, difficult as the search for unity in Paul's thought may be, it seems at least highly improbable that anyone should engage in the massive kind of double-think that Pfleiderer suggests. It is more likely that Paul has modified some of the notions which he has taken over in ways which minimize contradictions. What is required, then, is some account of the kinds of changes which Paul may have effected. This would include an account of how notions drawn from the relevant religious systems interact with and modify one another.

Similar problems are raised by the handling of Jesus' teaching by the History of Religions school. Once again members of this school tended to isolate two strands in Jesus' teaching: one broadly traditional Jewish and ethical which addressed itself to men as capable of responding to ethical injunctions; the other apocalyptic, calling men to repent in face of the coming judgement and intervention of God in men's affairs. While it was certainly recognized that within these strands Jesus had made significant modifications, for example, in respect of ritual and ceremonial Jewish laws and in relation to the crasser materialistic and nationalistic hopes associated with Jewish apocalyptic, there was considerable doubt as to how the two strands could be reconciled, other than by some literary solution or by playing down one side or the other. Again the problem lies with the tacit assumption that the key concepts which figure in Jesus' teaching are drawn with little or no modification from the traditions by which he was influenced. While this assumption could be true, it should not be a presupposition of inquiry. There are other lines of interpretation which locate the primary thrust of Jesus' teaching in the ways in which he changed traditional concepts.

II

We turn now to a more detailed discussion of how these general considerations bear on the practical problems of interpreting the teaching of Jesus. First we shall illustrate some of the limitations of scholarly work in this area by considering two contributions, one early, the other quite recent. We shall then pass via discussion of Martin Hengel's work on the Zealots to offer some constructive suggestions on the topic in hand.

Johannes Weiss's *Die Predigt Jesu vom Reiche Gottes*, particularly in its second edition of 1900,[6] has by general agreement largely determined the terms of subsequent debate on the subject. It serves to illustrate both the strengths and limitations of the theoretical position of the History of Religions school to which it is clearly indebted. We shall focus on the opening section of the second edition, 'Old Testament and Jewish Models of the Idea of the Kingdom of God' (op. cit., pp. 1–35).

According to Weiss '[t]he message of the nearness of the Kingdom of God, with which Jesus begins his public ministry, is as he [Jesus] understands it the announcement of the *messianic age*' (p. 1). But why, Weiss asks, did Jesus choose expressions pertaining to the Kingdom of God to announce the messianic age? Clearly his choice must have been determined by consideration for his hearers but it should not simply be assumed that the concept of the Kingdom of God as understood by Jesus is identical with the concept of the messianic age as it occurs in the Old Testament and in Judaism generally. Yet just this assumption has led scholars to read into Jesus' concept of the Kingdom 'a range of conceptions and expressions which have a quite different origin and form' (p. 1) from those which are in fact primarily associated with it.

The question which Weiss raises is very much to the point. His inquiry is motivated right from the start by a quite proper perception of the need to track down the sense of the expressions which Jesus used as they occurred in communities which were contemporaneous with him. Thus Weiss proceeds to examine a range of Old Testament and Jewish expressions pertaining to the Kingdom of God.

His main conclusions are familiar enough. He claims that the idea of the Kingdom of God occurs in two main forms. In one of its forms the emphasis is upon God's rule as it is represented, or immanent, in the life of the community. This form is common in the Psalms and also in Rabbinic literature. Weiss endorsed the view, held by Dalman, that Jesus' preaching at Mark 10.15 and Matthew 13.52 contains expressions echoing Rabbinic formulae which articulate the notion of the Kingdom of God as a theocracy in which men submit themselves to God's rule and enjoy its blessings. All the same, Weiss thinks, the similarities are superficial. In Jesus' preaching, the concept of the Kingdom of God is eschatological, relating as it does to a decisive intervention of God which will overcome the present order and inaugurate a new age.

In the other main form of the idea of the Kingdom of God, the emphasis is rather on the transcendence of God's rule and thus on the sharp contrast between it and all earthly rule. This brings with it the thought that God's rule will become effective in the course of events only through divine intervention. In 1 Samuel, for example, God's kingship is set in opposition to human kingship, while in Deutero-Isaiah 52.7ff, the prophet looks forward, beyond the present suffering of the people of Israel, to a time when 'all the ends of the earth shall see the salvation of our God' (Isaiah 52.10). The theme of the transcendence of God's rule also occurs in Rabbinic literature. In the Targum to Obadiah (T. Ob. v. 21), for example, we find the belief that '[i]t is not enough . . . that men recognize God's rule and subordinate themselves to it: God must himself intervene and show himself as King, whether he actually establishes his sovereignty anew by powerful deeds or whether he merely "reveals" that he really is still king' (p. 16). In either case '[i]t is a question of the self-demonstration of God, and an intervention in the fortunes of men and a decisive turn which God gives to history' (pp. 16–17). Weiss suggests that, although in these respects the Rabbinic teaching is similar to the teaching of Jesus, there are, nevertheless, far deeper differences. For the Rabbis the coming of the Kingdom is the confirmation of something which is already essentially present. '[I]t comes down to the establishment of the Davidic Kingdom, to the liberation of the people and the restoration of its old glory' (p. 17). For Jesus, by contrast, the Kingdom of God is eschatological and can only be said to be present in so far as 'the end' is already on its way.

Neither in the Rabbinic teaching nor in Daniel, Enoch, Ezra or Baruch, all of which contain traces of the concept of the Kingdom with a definite emphasis on its transcendence, is there to be found the idea which, according to Weiss, is so central for the preaching of Jesus, namely that, with the coming of the Kingdom of God, the rule of Satan will be overthrown and destroyed (see, for example, Matthew 12.25–9). The dualist world-view presupposed by this idea is not, Weiss thinks, characteristic of the Old Testament, despite isolated hints in Isaiah 24—5. It is, he thinks, probably of Persian origin, deriving from the dualism of Zoroastrian teaching. However, it does feature prominently in the Assumption of Moses and in the Revelation of John and was no doubt part of the range of ideas occurring in the messianic Judaism of Jesus' time.

For Weiss the upshot of this discussion is that the greatness of Jesus lay not in the originality of his teaching but 'in the fact that he lived, fought and suffered for the conviction that the Kingdom of God was even now about to appear and to win the victory for ever' (p.35). The time has come, Weiss thinks, 'to discard the rationalist tendency to look for Jesus' significance in the originality of his ideas and doctrines. A freer and livelier historical perspective will take it for granted that the new religion follows the forms of thought and modes of expression of its time' (pp. 34–5).

For our present purposes, it is not necessary to take issue with all of Weiss's historical and interpretative judgements. Our aim is rather to highlight the methodological limitations of his approach and to suggest interpretative possibilities which it obscures. Our comments illustrate the main themes of section I concerning the importance of linguistic and conceptual change and the network characteristics of systems of thought and their linguistic articulations.

As we have seen, from the claim that there are analogies between the thought underlying Jesus' preaching and that of certain contemporary Jewish writings with a dualistic world view, Weiss infers that Jesus' teaching is not original. However, the suppressed premise which this inference requires is obviously false, namely that these *analogies* are indicative of identity or close similarity in thought. A speaker or writer can employ familiar linguistic forms in new ways to express new thoughts while retaining the 'core' of their customary content. Whether he does or not can only be determined by examining them in the light of whatever else the speaker or writer has to say.

Weiss does from time to time acknowledge this. He recognizes, for example (p. 7), that Jesus could quite self-consciously have used a Rabbinic formula about receiving the Kingdom of God while according it a sense significantly different from that which it had for the Rabbis. If he does not apply the general principle underlying this point to those sayings in Jesus' preaching for which he finds analogues in the Assumption of Moses, it is perhaps because he does not press far enough the other theme recalled above, namely the importance of the network characteristics of systems of thought and their linguistic articulations. Weiss is quite properly concerned to elucidate ideas by locating them within 'chains of thought' (*Gedankenreihen*, p. 19). This is what leads him to discriminate two major forms of the idea of the Kingdom of God. He is not sufficiently attentive, however, to the fact that Jesus' preaching of the Kingdom, even where it contains vivid apocalyptic imagery, should be read in the light of his other teaching on, for example, ethics and even, as we would suggest, on purity.[7] The latter Weiss sees as being largely unrelated to Jesus' main religious doctrine (p. 137). As to the former, while Weiss does recognize that Jesus' command to love one's enemies is connected to his preaching of the Kingdom, he does not take it to illuminate the content of that preaching. Such commands, he thinks, are not about 'lasting social relationships and coming to terms with one's opponents . . . but the instructions for the last days of the struggle when the divine judge will all too soon put an end to all human strife' (p. 150). Now this may, in fact, be so, but before concluding that it is, we ought, at least, to raise the question whether Jesus' ethical teaching, which on the face of it seems to be concerned with this world, does not reveal something important about the content of Jesus' preaching, about what for him was the nature of God's Kingdom and the *manner* of God's exercise of his power. Inquiry along these lines might be expected to offset the unfortunate tendency, which Weiss imparted to scholarship in this field, to subordinate considerations about the content of the notion of the Kingdom of God to considerations about when Jesus believed the Kingdom was or would be revealed or established.

It is interesting to compare Weiss's work with recent work in the field by Bruce Chilton. In his book *God in Strength* Chilton, like Weiss, reveals a preoccupation with sources.[8] His primary concern, however, is not so much to show that Jesus' preaching is a product of its time as to uncover and interpret authentic sayings of Jesus. He examines eleven passages in the synoptic Gospels and attempts to analyse their diction with a view to identifying both the Evangelists' redactional contributions and the linguistic and theological provenance of the traditional material which is uncovered when the Evangelists' contributions have been removed. Chilton claims to have identified 'a primitive logia stratum with consistent linguistic traits and a distinctive theology' (p. 279). His methodological strategy is to look for analogies of thought content and linguistic structure between those parts of the Gospel sayings under investigation which he thinks are traditional and material from elsewhere which could conceivably be representative of the sort of thought and language which influenced Jesus. On finding, for example, that the notions of fulfilment, the nearing of the Kingdom, repentance and believing in the gospel, which occur in the traditional components of Mark 1.15 also occur in the Targum to Isaiah in distinctively similar patterns of thought and expressed in distinctively similar linguistic form, Chilton infers that these elements of Mark 1.15 have their source in the Targums. He then suggests on stylistic grounds that the material in question is dominical. The same technique is applied to the traditional and arguably dominical elements of other key passages in the synoptic tradition. Chilton concludes that Jesus' preaching of the Kingdom should be understood in the light of the Targums and, more specifically, in the light of their view of the coming of the Kingdom as the saving revelation of God himself (p. 283).

There is much in Chilton's methodology which requires critical scrutiny. It raises difficult questions about the criteria for selecting key passages for investigation and for distinguishing traditional from redactional material.[9] Our main criticism, however, does not so much concern Chilton's claim to have identified dominical sayings and their roots. It has rather to do with his further assumption that the theologies of Jesus and the Targums, with respect to the Kingdom of God, are significantly similar – similar enough to regard the Targums as of primary importance for the interpretation of Jesus' preaching. The problem here is in essence the same as that which we have already found in Weiss's discussion: analogies between patterns of thought are taken to be indicative of fundamental affinities. To be sure Chilton pays far more attention than Weiss does to analogies between linguistic structures and these may well provide him with a sounder basis for his claim to have identified the sources of Jesus' thought and language. But, as we have repeatedly stressed, in view of the possibilities of deliberate linguistic and conceptual change, sources are not necessarily the primary determinants of content and thus not necessarily the primary constraint on interpretation.

At the end of the day, Chilton has remarkably little to say on the content of Jesus' preaching. Notwithstanding the value of his inquiry into sources, we are still left with questions about what God's self-revelation amounts to, about what sorts of power and strength he manifests and about what exactly those who look forward to the coming of his Kingdom expect to happen. After all, the vision of Isaiah and the Targum to Isaiah 50 presents a quite different picture from that which the synoptic records associate with the coming of the Kingdom when, for example, they depict Jesus as having meals with tax collectors and sinners. Again, we see the importance of appreciating the network characteristics of systems of thought and their expression, which means in this case being prepared to interpret Jesus' preaching of the Kingdom in the light of other aspects of his teachings and, indeed, in the light of his actions.

III

As we noted earlier in section I, theological beliefs have implications for what people do or could experience and implications for how they should act. These implications exhibit the content of the beliefs. We should therefore expect to find clues to the interpretation of the theology of a particular group in the ways in which the group responded to prevailing social and political circumstances. What they believe will be reflected in their interpretation of and feelings about these circumstances and in their prescriptions for change. Inquiries along these lines should be expected to illuminate both the changing content of beliefs and the ways in which they both influence and respond to their social and political setting. For an account of beliefs about the Kingdom of God in Palestine from the time of Herod I until around AD 70 which does attend both to their changing pattern and to their social and political setting, we turn to Martin Hengel's great study *Die Zeloten*.[10]

Hengel is concerned to portray the developments and changes in religious beliefs which underlay Jewish armed resistance to increasingly oppressive Roman rule. For Hengel, the theological foundations of the Zealot movement are laid by Judas the Galilean. Judas taught that since God alone is King, the Jews should bear allegiance only to him and therefore should neither pay taxes nor submit to the census of Cyrenius. Rather they should strive for freedom and follow their charismatic prophetic leaders in a holy war against the Romans.

This Jewish liberation movement is a puzzling phenomenon. As Hengel points out, the doctrine of Judas 'broke with a centuries old tradition of dominance by foreign overlords which the Jews had borne relatively willingly from the time of the destruction of Jerusalem to the reign of Antiochus Epiphanes' (p. 94). Hengel seeks to explain how this came about by showing how God's kingship came to be understood in such a way that the belief that God alone is King could serve as a reason for resistance to Roman rule. After all it is not at all obvious that this belief need either conflict with allegiance to earthly rulers in general or require violent resistance to the Romans. According to Hengel, three major factors contribute to Judas' understanding of God's kingship.

There were tensions within Jewish thought about the Kingdom of God which Judas may be seen as resolving. In particular, there was the tension between thinking of the Kingdom of God, on the one hand, in terms of the imminent rule of God and his people, and on the other hand, in terms of the ever-present rule of God proclaimed in the cult (p. 96). Judas overcame this tension by seeking to reduce the difference between the two views. Through armed revolt against Roman rule, and through his call to unswerving allegiance to God alone, he sought, in effect, to make the present conform to the vision of a world effectively ruled by God and his people, a strategy which would at the same time, if successful, minimize the clash between that vision and the actual circumstances which prevailed (p. 148).

The way for Judas' understanding of God's kingship was paved by changes in Jewish nomenclature for God which went hand in hand with changes in the concept of God. The material which Hengel gathers together (pp. 98ff) shows a growing tendency for Jews to adopt names for God drawn from oriental court language. Names such as 'King of Kings', 'Lord', 'despot', 'dynast', and the like, represent God as an oriental potentate with absolute power. Hengel suggests that the creed which Josephus ascribed to Judas and his followers to the effect that God is sole leader and master[11] 'is merely a final consequence of the . . . general Jewish view that God is the sovereign Ruler of the World and, in particular, is the Lord of Israel' (p. 102).

At the same time as the Jews were affirming their belief in the absolute power of God in terms drawn from the oriental courts, they were encountering the force of imperial and political power. Hengel suggests that for the Jews one of the most objectionable manifestations of Roman power would have been the assertion of the divine status of the Emperor. In the year in which Octavian had adopted the title 'Augustus' (Sebastos), Herod renamed the town Samaria 'Sebaste' and erected there a temple for Caesar (p. 106). In the light of developments such as these, Judas' teaching becomes intelligible. 'Impressed as they were by the increasing divinization of the earthly ruler of the world, Judas and his followers proclaimed the unlimited rule of God in the political realm as well' (p. 102).

Hengel's analysis both illustrates, and is itself illuminated by, the interpretative perspective which we have urged. In calling upon the Jews to acknowledge that God alone is King, Judas drew upon ancient Jewish tradition concerning God's kingship. Yet it is only in the light of those more recent shifts in the understanding of God's kingship, which Hengel charts, and in the light of contemporary social and political developments, that we can see how acknowledging that God alone is King could have the practical implications which it had for Judas and his followers. On this Hengel is surely right; but more needs to be said on the explanatory connection between the shifts in understanding and the social and political context on the one hand, and the practical implications on the other. As viewed by Hengel, the former led to the latter via the recognition that God's unlimited rule extended to the political realm *as well*. (See the quotation above, p. 102.) The difficulty with this is that presumably no Jew would have doubted that *in some sense* God's rule always had extended to the political realm – that earthly kingdoms only function by divine sufferance. The crucial point, which Hengel does not make explicit but which is suggested by his discussion, is that the explanatory factors he adduces bring in their train a shift in the understanding of what it is for God to rule over the political realm. Thus it was not so much the recognition that God ruled in the political realm that was new but rather the conception of what that rule amounted to. The changes in nomenclature, which Hengel charts, promoted a concept of God according to which God has the kind of authority and power which earthly rulers have. Judas possessed just such a concept. That is why from the claim that God alone is King, he inferred that people ought to obey God to the exclusion of obedience to earthly rulers. But, as Hengel suggests, Judas would have been influenced also by that element in Jewish thought which sees God's reign as being established here and now. His military action was therefore not merely in obedience to what he took to be a divine command. It was an attempt to make the present turn out in the way that would be expected if God's reign really were effective in the political realm.

The methodological lessons to be drawn from this discussion can be summarized as follows. To understand a concept such as that of the kingship of God or of the Kingdom of God, as it is employed by a community, one must be able to locate it in a network of concepts which for that community is constitutive of its content. In locating a concept in a network, one will often have to look for logical connections between beliefs involving the concept and beliefs which pertain to the observable world. The distinction between linguistic expressions and their senses or contents is crucial since sameness of expression does not guarantee sameness of sense. This is one reason why the force of Judas' message required explanation.

Perhaps the reluctance of many biblical scholars to relate theological concepts and beliefs to what people can quite literally see and feel around them can be traced to the false assumption that such an approach is in some unacceptable way reductionist. We can distinguish here two kinds of reductionism, one conceptual, the other explanatory. Conceptual reductionism requires that the content of all matter of fact beliefs is exhausted by their empirical content. Explanatory reductionism seeks to explain why people adopt general world views or ideologies (including under these headings systems of religious belief) in terms of beliefs and desires pertaining to the physical environment. On the approach to interpretation which we are commending, theological beliefs certainly have a bearing on the empirical world and this is relevant to an understanding of their content. But neither this nor Hengel's historical analysis requires commitment to either type of reductionism.

It is interesting to note here that the East German Marxist scholar, Heinz Kreissig, has criticized Hengel for explaining political developments in Judaism exclusively in terms of developments in religious belief. Hengel's method, Kreissig thinks, is unscientific because it amounts to a search for an Old Testament text for every event in Judea and ignores acute problems of the time.

Kreissig's own view in his *Die sozialen Zusammenhänge des judäischen Krieges* is that religious development can be properly explained only in terms of economic conflicts and interests.[12] The upheavals of Jewish society under Roman rule which led to the Jewish war were, he thinks, principally the result of conflicts between town and country dwellers, between tenants and landlords and between rich and poor in a situation of serious economic pressure. The Zealot theology was merely the ideological dressing of their real motivation which was economic.

Kreissig's criticism of Hengel is hardly just. Far from ignoring 'acute problems of the time', Hengel, as we have seen, brings out the ways in which religious beliefs developed in response to, and also influenced, the course of events. Hengel, that is, does not subscribe to the explanatory reductionism which appears to be implicit in Kreissig's approach and brings with it its own particular difficulties. The explanatory factors upon which Kreissig relies seem unlikely to account for the diversity of theological and practical responses within Judaism or for the fact that elsewhere in the Empire resistance was rare. Moreover, even if Kreissig's explanatory reductionism were plausible, it would still be necessary to account for how it was possible for Judas and his followers to rationalize armed resistance in the way that they did, and this would require just the kind of examination of changes in concepts and beliefs and the unravelling of their content which Hengel's analysis provides.

IV

Let us now return to the consideration of Jesus' teaching and preaching in the light of the discussion so far. In our comments on Weiss and Chilton, we stressed the importance of attempting to understand Jesus' teaching about the Kingdom against the background of other aspects of his teaching. These other aspects could be of importance in grasping what the coming of the Kingdom was believed by Jesus to consist in and thus could shed light on the continuities and discontinuities between what Jesus said about the Kingdom and the diverse beliefs held by other groups of contemporary Jews.[13] This is the general approach taken by John Riches in his *Jesus and the Transformation of Judaism*. We shall attempt to show here how its main thesis accords with this general theoretical perspective.

Jesus announced the Kingdom of God as already present in his preaching and deeds. Chilton's study interestingly corroborates this but, as we have noted, does not provide us with a developed analysis of what for Jesus God's power or strength amounted to, and so fails to bring out the *differences* between Jesus' preaching and the theology of the Targums. Notwithstanding the analogies between Jesus' thought and language and various elements of contemporary Judaism, there are grounds for thinking that Jesus substantially reworked the notion of God's power. In the Targum to Isaiah, the revelation of God's Kingdom is linked to the nations' being counted as a destruction before him (40.7), or being utterly destroyed (60.12; cf. 60.1), or with Zion's being satisfied with the riches of the peoples and delighting in the spoils of their kings (60.16).[14] Among the Zealots, God's Kingdom is viewed as a world theocracy which can be appropriately furthered by taking up arms against Rome and her agents. These notions are quite different from those found in Jesus' teaching. For Jesus, the Kingdom was manifested in acts of healing, forgiveness and acceptance of the outcast and the enemy. This comes out clearly when his teaching on the Kingdom is considered in relation to, for example, his sharing meals with tax collectors and sinners.[15]

In the Old Testament and later Judaism, meals are acts of fellowship which also have a wide range of religious associations.[16] Sacrificial meals might be held as acts of expiation or as acts of communion with Jahweh or, as in the case of the Passover, as commemorations of Jahweh's great deeds of redemption.[17] Such meals would reaffirm the bond between God and his people. At a later period, meals became the focus of various renewal groups, notably the *ḥaburoth*[18] and Qumran,[19] and the expected fulfilment of Israel's hopes came to be connected with a messianic banquet.[20] Given the religious associations of celebratory meals and Jesus' announcement of the Kingdom as already present in his preaching and deeds, it is reasonable to suppose that his meals with tax-gatherers and sinners are indicative of what he took to be the nature of the final communion which was to be established between God and his people.[21] If this is so, then one can understand the outrage which they occasioned when the expectations to which they bore witness conflicted sharply with those of many

Jews. The conflict is clearest in relation to the expectation that, with the coming of the Kingdom, God's enemies both inside and outside Israel would be overthrown and punished. By contrast with this, Jesus' sharing of meals with outcasts and collaborators speaks powerfully of God's forgiveness and acceptance of them. The same may be said of Jesus' healings and exorcisms which, in the context of his preaching and the understanding of the time, are indicative of his associating God's power with the liberation of those in bondage to Satan and his agents, and with finding the lost and healing the sick.[22]

The significance of Jesus' sharing of meals with sinners for understanding the content of his preaching of the Kingdom is further brought out by consideration of the purity regulations which for some groups governed both diet and eating.[23] The *ḥaberim* observed and developed regulations governing diet and handwashing which would have made sharing meals with less strictly observant Jews difficult.[24] Qumran had a more elaborately structured society with even greater barriers between it and the outside world.[25] Its needs were protected by detailed regulations concerning entry, rank, purification and the like. Access to its meals marked an important stage in entry to the community.[26] The hierarchical structure of the community itself determined some of its regulations about pollution: if a junior member touched a senior member at a meal, the senior was polluted.[27] In the teaching of Qumran, of the *ḥaberim* and of the Pharisees, God's Kingdom and power were linked to his holiness. In Qumran, the community's worship was equated with the worship of the Temple, the place where God's presence and glory was manifested.[28] Conformity to the purity regulations thus flowed from an understanding of God as one who rules in holiness, whose power and presence show him to be separated from all that is alien to him, and who demands of those who worship him that they too separate themselves from all that is alien, that is, from Gentiles, tax-gatherers, sinners and the like. The Pharisees similarly taught that fully to take on the yoke of the Kingdom involved purification: relieving oneself, washing, ritual vesting and then reciting certain prayers.[29] In effect, God's power and strength were understood to be manifested, for the time at least, in the sacred realm of private and family prayer, where Jews were separated and distinct from the world.

In the light of these considerations, there comes into view the interesting possibility that the meals which Jesus shared are significant not only for the understanding of his preaching of the Kingdom, but also as indicators of his having rejected traditional notions of purity outright. According to Mark 7.15 Jesus said, 'there is nothing outside a man which by going into him can defile him; but the things which come out of a man are what defile him'. This saying is sometimes thought to be so distinctive and so uncharacteristic of first-century Judaism that it must have originated in the early Church.[30] However, if the meals which Jesus shared are significant in the way suggested then the saying could arguably have come from Jesus himself. In favour of this are the facts that: it accords well with what we have seen of his preaching of the Kingdom; it clearly stands early in the tradition history of Mark;[31] and an attribution to the early Church is less, rather than more, likely in view of controversies within the Church concerning purity. Looked at in this way, Jesus' remarks on purity are not simply, as Weiss thought (op. cit., p. 137), part of a polemic against the hypocrisy of the Pharisees. On the contrary, they are intimately linked to his teaching on the Kingdom in virtue of their implication for the notions of holiness, separation, hierarchy, abomination and hatred.

Traditional notions of purity helped to maintain and reinforce boundaries between groups of people, in particular between those who conformed to the regulations governing purity and those who did not and, in hierarchically ordered communities such as Qumran, in addition, between different levels of the hierarchy. Jesus' rejection of these notions may thus be viewed as calling into question, indeed, as seeking to dismantle, these boundaries. But then his attitude to purity is a natural corollary of his ethical teaching. His teaching about humility and the servanthood of leaders and above all his injunction to love one's enemies find, that is, their counterpart in his rejection of traditional notions of purity, and reflect his understanding of God and his rule. His justification for loving one's enemies, that God lets his sun shine on both good and evil alike (Matthew 5.45), is of a piece with the openness of his invitation to the Kingdom. (Contrast Weiss, above, p. 47.)

These are just some of the interpretative hypotheses which naturally suggest themselves when we take seriously the need to look at Jesus' preaching of the Kingdom in the light of other aspects of his teaching and in the light of his actions. This is precisely what the methodological reflections which we have presented required us to do. Of course, we are then brought face to face with the question of how we determine which sayings in the synoptic records may be ascribed to Jesus.[32] Far from ignoring this question, our discussion actually points to factors which need to be taken into account in answering it. As we say in discussing Mark 7.15, the fact that a saying harmonizes with a body of sayings, which there are independent grounds for taking to be indicative of Jesus' teaching, counts in favour of the hypothesis that the saying in question, in respect of its content, is ascribable to Jesus. The kind of harmony which matters, however, has to do not just with superficial linguistic or literary features, though these are by no means irrelevant, but more importantly with patterns of thought. Exactly parallel considerations hold for the so-called principle of dissimilarity. It is commonly held that in order to determine which sayings are authentic to Jesus, we must first isolate a group of sayings which are sufficiently dissimilar to contemporary beliefs that they can be regarded as original to Jesus and then extend this group of sayings by adding others which harmonize with it. Where similarity or dissimilarity is concerned, again, what matters are patterns of thought. A group of sayings may be linguistically keyed to first-century Palestine and yet be radically distinct in respect of their content. This has been a recurring theme of this paper.

If we are right in holding that Jesus radically changed the concept of the Kingdom of God and, correspondingly, used expressions pertaining to the Kingdom with a sense radically different from, though nevertheless related to, that which they had in contemporary Judaism, then we have to reckon with the possibility that those who transmitted his utterances might on occasion have read into them implications which he himself rejected, implications which the linguistic conventions obtaining in other Jewish communities would have led one to expect.

For example, it is likely that those who transmitted Jesus' Kingdom utterances will have been vividly aware of those concepts which link God's kingship with the destruction of his enemies and their judgement. Consequently they may well have read Jesus' utterances in accordance with those concepts and built their readings into the texts in which they transmit his teaching. Chilton provides what may be an example of this (op. cit., pp. 179–201). He argues that Matt. 8.11, 12 (cf. Luke 13.28, 29) contains both a traditional stratum and a complex redactional overlay. The traditional saying 'many will come from the east and west and will sit down with Abraham, Isaac and Jacob in the Kingdom' has been supplemented by the further clause 'but the sons of the Kingdom will go out (be cast out) into outer darkness and there will be weeping and gnashing of teeth'. Chilton thinks that the supplementary clause for the most part derives from Q and Matthew. Whether or not this is so, it is the sort of thing one would expect if Jesus employed a concept of the Kingdom which was radically different from that of his contemporaries. Admittedly, this is not the only interpretation which the passage in question lends itself to. Perhaps what Chilton regards as redactional is in substance, if not in linguistic form, dominical, but should not be read in a literal way. Or perhaps though dominical, it shows that Jesus had not fully worked out the implications of his teaching on the Kingdom for the notion of judgement. Matters of interpretation such as these will in any case only be settled if scholars pay more attention than they customarily do to the relations between language, thought, experience and practice.

NOTES

1 The perspective outlined here is anticipated in J. Riches, *Jesus and the Transformation of Judaism* (*JTJ*), London 1980, and in A. Millar and J. K. Riches, 'Interpretation: A Theoretical Perspective and Some Applications', *Numen* xxviii, 1 (1981), pp. 29–53.

2 The corner quotes notation is fully explained by W. V. Quine in his *Mathematical Logic*, revised edn (Harper and Row, New York, 1962), chapter 1, section 6.

3 This and other relevant topics in the theory of meaning are examined in A. Millar 'Where's the Use in Meaning?' (*Dialectica*, forthcoming) and 'How Meanings are Attached to Expressions' (forthcoming).

4 O. Pfleiderer in his *Der Paulinismus. Ein Beitrag zur Geschichte der urchristlichen Theologie* (Leipzig 1873), p. 7, defines the problem as one of finding a common root '*aus* welcher sich sowohl der psychologische Prozess der Bekehrung Pauli, als auch die Genesis seines eigenthümlichen Evangeliums *erklären* liesse'. Cf. the account of the History of Religions School in W. G. Kümmel, *The New Testament. The History of the Investigation of its Problems* (London 1973), pp. 206–324.

5 'In all this we have found confirmed the expectations to which the Jewish-Greek education of Saul–Paul the Hellenist and Pharisee

naturally gave rise: the Pharisaic and Hellenistic ways of thinking formed two currents which in Paulinism flow through one channel, yet without being really united.' Quoted in Kümmel, op. cit., p. 209 from O. Pfleiderer, *Primitive Christianity, its literature and doctrine, described in historical inter-relationship*, London 1906.

6 1st edn, Göttingen 1892; 2nd edn fully revised, Göttingen 1900.

7 For suggestions along these lines, see section IV.

8 *God in Strength: Jesus' Announcement of the Kingdom, Studien zum Neuen Testament und seiner Umwelt*, Freistadt 1979.

9 In connection with the former, Chilton makes dubious inferences from the grammatical features of sentences to the logical structure of their content. See op. cit., pp. 14ff.

10 *Die Zeloten. Untersuchungen zur jüdischen Freiheitsbewegung in der Zeit von Herodes I bis 70 n Chr. Arbeiten zur Geschichte des antiken Judentums und des Urchristentums.* Bd 1, 1st edn, Leiden 1961; 2nd edn revised and enlarged, Leiden 1976.

11 Josephus, *Ant.* xviii, 23.

12 Berlin 1970. See p. 92 for the criticism of Hengel.

13 It should of course be stressed that attempts to account for the differences between Jesus' views and those of other contemporary groups are not necessarily apologetically motivated, as E. P. Sanders seems to suggest, *JSNT* 19 (1983), p. 22. Asking such questions is rather, one would have thought, an integral part of searching for the specific character of any historical personage.

14 G. Vermes in *Jesus and the World of Judaism* suggests, citing Isaiah 60.1–6, that Deutero- and Trito-Isaiah attest a concept of the kingdom 'with no associations whatever with violence or war.' (p. 34). Rather 'the manifestation of God's sovereignty over his own was to serve as a magnet to the rest.' (p. 35). He does not however discuss the verses in Isaiah 60 which allude to kings being led in procession into Jerusalem (v. 11) or to the laying waste of wide regions of those nations which refuse to serve Jerusalem (v. 12). Certainly submission to Jerusalem in Isaiah 60 seems a rather different thing to the proselyte's submission to Torah in Tanhuma (ed. Buber) I, p. 63, to which Vermes refers in this context.

15 *JTJ*, pp. 105–6. Cf. the very interesting discussion of the subject in E. P. Sanders, art. cit., pp. 20ff with much of which we are in substantial agreement.

16 See G. Fohrer, art. 'Mahlzeiten II', *RGG*[3], vol. iv, cols 670f.

17 See B. Hentschke, art. 'Opfer II', *RGG*[3], vol. iv, cols 1641ff; B. A. Levine, *In the Presence of the Lord*, Leiden 1974.

18 J. Neusner, 'The Fellowship in the Second Jewish Commonwealth', *HThR* 53 (1960), pp. 125–42; S. Westerholm, *Jesus and Scribal Authority*, Lund 1978, pp. 69–71; A. Oppenheimer, *The 'Am Haaretz*, Leiden 1977, pp. 51–62.

19 The literature is too extensive to detail here, but cf. W. Paschen, *Rein und Unrein, Studien zum Alten and Neuen Testament*, Munich 1970, esp. pp. 103–15.

20 Isaiah 25.6; Matthew 7.11f; 22.2–4; 26.29; Revelation 3.20; 19.9; IQSa II, 11–22.

21 Cf. the discussion of the historical reliability of the synoptic accounts of Jesus' meals in *JTJ*, pp. 101–3.

22 *JTJ*, p. 104.

23 *JTJ*, ch. 6. For an important discussion of the nature of purity regulations, see M. Douglas, *Purity and Danger*, London 1978, and J. Neusner, *The Idea of Purity in Ancient Judaism*, Leiden 1973. Cf. also Paschen, *Rein und Unrein*.

24 Oppenheimer, *The 'Am Ha-aretz*, pp. 61–2.

25 J. Maier, 'Zum Begriff *yaḥad* in den Texten von Qumran', in *ZAW* 72 (1960), pp. 162–5; G. Vermes, *The Dead Sea Scrolls in English*, London 1968, pp. 16–33.

26 IQS VI, 16f, in Vermes' translation; cf. Vermes, *Dead Sea Scrolls in English*, p. 27, but ctr Paschen, *Rein und Unrein*, pp. 95–6.

27 Josephus, *Bell.* II, 150.

28 IQS 5.6: 8.4–10; 9.3–6; cf. Paschen, *Rein und Unrein*, pp. 134–52.

29 B. Berakoth, 146.15a: the saying attributed to R. Johanan ben Zakkai, 'If one desires to accept upon himself the yoke of the kingdom in the most perfect manner, he should relieve himself and wash his hands and put on *tephillin* and recite the Shema[c]' and say the tephillah: this is the complete acknowledgement of the kingdom of heaven.'

30 Those who oppose the originality to Jesus of Mark 7.15 include E. Schweizer, *The Good News According to Mark*, London 1971, pp. 146, 149; S. Schulz, 'Die neue Frage nach dem historischen Jesus' in *Neues Testament und Geschichte*, Festschrift for O. Cullmann, 1972, pp. 33ff. See the discussion in W. G. Kümmel, 'Äussere und innere Reinheit des Menschen bei Jesus', in *Heilsgeschehen und Geschichte*, vol. ii, Marburg 1978, pp. 117–29.

31 See *JTJ*, p. 217, n. 70.

32 See *JTJ*, p. 54, where the point is made less sharply.

4

Taking up the Cross and Turning the Cheek

J. DUNCAN M. DERRETT

Introduction

That the believer should take up and carry a cross, and that he should turn the other cheek are two of the incredible sayings of Jesus. Let us make sense of them, together, for they belong together.[1] The astounding saying, approximately 'Take up one's cross', meaning one's peculiar cross, found in different forms (Mark 8.34 par.; Matthew 10.38; Ev. Thom. 55; Luke 14.27), can hardly be an injunction to seek crucifixion. This prospect can recruit none but the neurotic. It calls no one to surrender to death in some cabbalistic ecstasy. Exposure of an executed corpse was, true enough, part of the penalty for idolatry and blasphemy known to the Jews,[2] and could be carried out where they had a free hand, but one wonders whether the saying *could* have meant 'take the risk that your fellow Jews will treat you so'. The saying, after all, is not propounded as a matter of taking a *risk*. Rather it is a peculiar commendation of asceticism. *Denial of self* (an allusion to the optimistic passage beginning at Job 42.6) is its *precondition*. The *purpose* is to follow Jesus, in life, emphasized by the double use of 'follow' (*akolouthein*) at Mark 8.34.

Some attempt to deprive the saying of any real force (the process ably satirized by Tolstoy) can be detected. By the eighteenth century it meant hardly more than 'bear with an irksome burden', whatever that might be.[3] The process goes very far back. We do not know when *aras ton stauron* was intruded into Mark 10.21, where Huck–Greeven actually print it now.[4] A glance at the context will show that this would have been impossible had the true meaning of the saying been known. Self-sought poverty is certainly not a, nor the, cross; nor is misfortune a precondition for 'taking it up', whatever that may be: only *self-denial* is. A reader of the enigmatic texts, which, if they were to have a clear single meaning, could as well have been unambiguous from the start, cannot pass 'take up his cross', or 'take up the cross' without the impression that one has a choice whether to bear the burden or not. One volunteers to assume a burden which, however, is not there (for the carrying) by one's own choice. It is not a matter of *inevitable necessity*, so we have something very subtle to consider.

Exploration below the texts reveals something easy enough to grasp, but not easy to accept. 'Taking up a cross', a picturesque technical term, implies (as we shall see) assuming the penalty for being a sinner, in the hopes of proceeding towards the Land of the Promise, an allegory for the world to come (Mark 10.30; Matthew 12.32). One who moved in that direction was secure in this very life (Matthew 28.20; cf. John 5.21, 24).

We are familiar with losing one's life in order to save it (Mark 8.35–7; cf. Job 13.13–16; Jeremiah 15.18–21).[5] The saying about the cross is not only near to this in the text but parallel to it in meaning. One 'crucifies' the body to save the soul. Since Jewish anthropology did not distinguish soul and body fundamentally, what we have is a concept of discipline, for we can neglect the rhetorical pseudo-distinction between 'person' and 'self' (both are, in the Hebrew, *nefeš*). Discipline of the soul (*askēsis*) was well known[6] and respected as a form of heroism: it appertained to Everyman (Mark 8.34, 'calling the *crowd*'; see Joel 3.5 LXX) who will run that race,[7] giving no pre-eminence to any 'professional' ascetic.

'Discipline' is a key to this early Christian teaching. A disposition is required, manifesting itself in behaviour. There is the no less extraordinary saying 'Resist not evil' (Matthew 5.39), with its famous illustration that one 'turns the other cheek'. Apart from the anomaly of nonviolent resistance, amply illustrated from stories both of Jesus and of Paul, there is the problem that if violence is to be eschewed, quite apart from psychiatric implications arising from the repression of natural resentments, the taking up of a *cross* is a curious procedure. Again the illustrations of the precept are eccentric. Is being pestered for a loan an 'evil'? Perhaps to some! James 4.7 and 1 Peter 5.9 enjoin upon us resistance to evil, and practical considerations have conspired to water down Matthew 5.39 into insignificance.[8]

It can be argued however that working principles for the Church have been communicated in an artful series of precepts each based upon three criteria, the behaviour of God (see Matthew 5.9, 45, 48, adapting Leviticus 19.2; Deuteronomy 18.13), the behaviour of biblical 'saints', and the behaviour of Christ, who definitively satisfied God's requirements. To work this out, particularly in the very compressed and suggestive antitheses of the Sermon on the Mount,[9] is somewhat of a challenge, and produces startling results. The old view, that Jesus abandoned the Yahweh of the Old Testament in favour of a deity of his own creation, needs to be modified, on various grounds: and one must bear in mind that even a superficial knowledge of the Old Testament confirms that Yahweh has his own, quite specific and illuminating position on slaying, anger, mocking, reconciliation, adultery, divorce, swearing (Yahweh's oath is the basis of Judaism), vengeance, and loving-kindness! The pattern which Yahweh manifested, and partially revealed in so many words to Moses, can, *properly interpreted with reference to time and place*, be followed propitiously, on the principle of imitation, by believers in Jesus (Ephesians 4.32; 5.1).

Meanwhile Mark's Gospel, which Matthew follows, was composed on a screen or model consisting of the story of the first trek.[10] Hosea 2.16–20 (EV 14–18) explains that the Children of Israel will one day retrace the steps of Joshua and at last achieve what Moses, and he, failed to do. Micah 6.5 shows how highly Yahweh valued the achievement of leading the remnant of Israel past Peor/Shittim to Gilgal. Jesus according to Mark retraced those steps, stage by stage, and, having done so, underwent the afflictions of Lamentations. Both Matthew (as Doeve saw)[11] and Luke (as Evans saw)[12] were compiled with an eye to books of the Torah neglected by Mark (Leviticus, Deuteronomy). We need not explain all that now; it suffices to recognize the very great advantage for Jewish hearers of the gospel to have a running gloss consisting in their preacher's allegories on the Hexateuch. He would bring out, what is implicit in Mark, namely Jesus' 'escalation' (to borrow E. Earle Ellis's happy phrase) in comparison with the ambiguous achievements of his less illustrious predecessors. The Old Testament 'authorities' behind our own conundrums were indeed observed by that genius Hugo Grotius (1644) and by John Mill (1707), but they could not draw the appropriate inferences from them.

Taking up a Cross

The stake that is to be taken up is to be used for the crucifixion of its carrier as and when necessary.[13] He must be ready to mount (*epibainein*) that which he has been carrying (*bastazein*): that is his part. In Mark's day, so far as we know, no one was crucified for being a Christian.[14] Jesus' experience was the sequel to total submission to the divine will (Mark 14.36). The persecution suffered by him and his followers, an idea prominent in Mark (10.30 *diōgmōn*), is the world's intolerance of their behaviour-pattern, sustained by a disposition, itself achieved by the cross-carrying.[15] The cross is no talisman; it signalizes the path which Christ trod *in life*. The merit he achieved in life is analogous to the merit Christian Everyman can, with effort, achieve: they are of the same kind.

Matthew refines and narrows the Marcan saying. The churchman takes up his cross as a first-class follower of Jesus. He participates in his sufferings and merits (Matthew 10.41) as compensation for rejecting the world. He leads a consecrated, and segregated, life. 'Taking a cross' means defying the world and so obtaining the Church's approbation (possibly Ev. Thom. 55 has the same aroma). Denying oneself has become a social rejection of unconverted relatives at least. One so qualifies for resurrection (see Matthew 16.24 in the light of 16.21). Luke agrees that the cross must be shouldered (Luke 14.27), but it must be taken up daily (9.23), so that the believer ever models himself anew upon an idealized Christ (cf. 19.17). Martyrdom is not contemplated. One must not be ashamed (cf. Jeremiah 17.13–18) of Christ's sacrifice, which purchased redemption.

The saying from Q is about *worthiness*, but no direct explanation is given us. The Marcan form has neither explanation nor illustration. The metaphor was to be expounded by a preacher, fortified by living tradition. Two different applications were contemplated by Matthew. In his day, as in Mark's, explanatory material must have been available from the Old Testament: whence else? The Diatessaron actually called in Isaiah 9.6!

We soon find the cross in the Old Testament. M. Wilcox convincingly explained what is true, that crucifixion was not alien to the thought-world or to the experience of Jews, however much such a penalty might be deprecated by Pharisees reforming native Jewish law.[16] Folk-memory read back crucifixion into several biblical events, crucifixion understood rather widely, the Roman method being only an example. Impaling was taken (as surviving Targums show) as a form of crucifixion. The form of disposal of the victim was less important than the occasion. If we ignore the less significant instance at Ezra 6.11, several Old Testament personages underwent this fate. What have they in common? According to Symmachus's rendering of Numbers 25.4 the Jews beguiled on the advice of Balaam into idolatry were crucified,[17] and this sets the pattern. It is a pattern we can perceive in several ancient, but post-biblical sources, each consistent with another.

The victims of crucifixion or impalement were in every case idolaters. Jesus was a second Joshua, commissioned to 'settle' the land. Legend tells how he gave the inhabitants a choice: submit, or be destroyed. Those who remained and declined to submit took the honourable course of resorting to arms. The consequences for Jericho and Ai were grievous (Joshua 8.29). Allegorists naturally explained the unedifying proceedings benevolently. Israelites would obtain their 'inheritance' in such a style because the land was tired of its inhabitants (Leviticus 18, 20) on account of their abominations which they practised in defiance of the Noachide laws.[18] The detailed procedure of dealing with prisoners, hanging them up before the Lord, taking them down from their 'trees' and burying them before sunset (Joshua 8.29, 10.26 relying on Deuteronomy 21.23, and thus germane to the *Heilsgeschichte*), was appropriate to the crime of defying the divine laws against immorality and idolatry, themselves intimately associated notions (Leviticus 17.7).

Joshua defeated, in turn, explicitly, a series of *kings*. The high point was the hanging of the five kings (see Joshua 10). While these were confined to a cave, Israel was successful and blameless. Obviously they must be permanently suppressed. Israel's feet were placed on their necks (Deuteronomy 33.29 LXX, Tgg; Psalms 91.13; 110.1; Leviticus R. X.7); and then the unhappy kings were hanged, and so on. Their corpses were thrown back into their cave, stoppered with stones. The story was evidently allegorical when written.

The five kings have 'ancestors'. Each of the five kings of Sodom, and so on (Genesis 14), was a specialist in his own vice.[19] The abominations of Canaan were not rooted out under Abraham and remained for Joshua's attention. Compromises with idolaters were forbidden (Exodus 23.32, Deuteronomy 7.2); yet within the land undefeated and unsubdued heathen remained. Moses had destroyed the five kings of Midian (Num. 31.8), but other fives survived. Five kings of the Philistines long pestered Israel (Joshua

13.3). Remnants of the nations remained (Joshua 13.13; 16.10) and Israel went a-whoring after their gods. The position was no different in Jesus' time, if the allegory is to be sustained.

The five kings are five forms of 'idolatry' corresponding to the five senses[20] (see John 4.17–18). The senses and their activities are distributed over the body, without reference to the nervous system. If the eye sins the eye must be repressed, if the hand the hand, etc. Leviticus 18.29 tells how those who practise abominations will be cut off (*krt*), and it is a neat idea that by self-amputation (known to penal law in Palestine!)[21] one can cut off only the offending part and save the remainder for the world to come (Mark 9.43; Matthew 5.27–30). One suffers rather than conform to the abominations of the nations. It is after all the fault of the five senses that the kings resisted Joshua. In the persons of the five kings the five senses, then enemies of Yahweh, were placed under his feet. The appropriate sequel was to kill them and hang them or to kill them by hanging them. One can indeed put a stop to 'passions warring in one's members' (James 4.1). The publicity of the act (cf. Colossians 2.15) provided a triumph conducive to conquest of the remainder.

Let us suppose the kings took up their crosses: that is what Plutarch, in an invaluable passage, suggests.[22] It may be objected that they did so involuntarily. There is no suggestion in Joshua that they benefited. But their crucifixions ended the qualities of rebellion against Yahweh which had infected the Israelites, notoriously susceptible after the Peor/Shittim episode. Vices threatening the host were neutralized. Though Jesus' recruiting attempted[23] to provide better prospects, Jesus' own crucifixion itself proved that ultimate humiliation and 'exhibition' of the vices in a defeated state was necessary to protect the whole people in their homeland. The follower of Christ must be aware of the inherited susceptibility to rebelliousness and carry a cross for himself as long as he walks through the world which is 'Egypt' and idolatrous 'Canaan' rolled into one. The theory that Jesus was a revolutionary and did not undergo crucifixion willingly – but rather had a salvation-myth fathered upon him *ex post facto* – must be regarded as completely exploded,[24] and therefore the positive evaluation of cross-carrying is as old as Jesus himself.

Origen[25] and Jerome,[26] both well briefed on Jewish traditions, knew this was how the five kings should be understood; it has been traditional in the Church thereafter.[27] A carol preserves allusion to the kings' role.[28] J. H. Michaelis in his *Biblia Hebraica*[29] related Romans 6.12–14 to the kings in their cave, and Joshua 10.22 to Luke 19.27 (the ruler's vengeance). Thus we are ready with a metaphor to take up the prophecy in Lamentations which bears directly on our point.

Lamentations can bear a dynamic interpretation, which can be detected already in the gory details of 2 Maccabees and 4 Maccabees. The versions of the Targum at Lamentations 3.27 (independent versions testifying to an ancient *Vorlage*) still show that the 'yoke' which a youth should take up implies afflictions which come upon him for the sake of the Name, sent by Yahweh in respect of light sins, so that he may have consideration for the sinner, lift them from him, and grant him salvation for the world to come.[30] One suffers for one's sins and those of one's fathers. Suffering provides a vicarious atonement.[31] The *ethnos* bears co-responsibility. The 'elect' must assume the yoke, recognizing and accepting suffering. Oppressors impose a suffering which is deserved (see various readings of Lamentations 3.7 LXX in the light of Jeremiah 35.14 LXX). Enemies of Israel, Yahweh's agents, will humiliate and impoverish her. She must accept this.

In the fifth dirge's climax the prince (*sārim*, honorific plural) will be hung by his hands (Lamentations 5.12), he (it is the Messiah) who was to have been Israel's protection amongst the heathen (Lamentations 4.20). The young men will then labour, struggle under, and faint upon the *wood* (Lamentations 5.13b, cf. versions). They are crucified and they carry wood, as the blind man of Bethsaida said he saw men like trees walking.[32] The climax of humiliation and degradation is to suffer the fate of the abominable Canaanites who became hewers of wood and drawers of water (cf. Mark 14.13). After these sufferings Yahweh will draw near to them and they to him, and all will be restored as in days of old (Lamentations 5.20–22). The sins of Israel are at last atoned for.

To take up the cross is to discipline the body with its passions,[33] to extirpate idolatry. The elect follow the prince. They too stumble and faint (*ekpnein*). Israel will be reunited with her deity. Crucifixion put sin to death,[34] and to that process no resistance whatever must be offered.

Resisting Evil

Hebrew and Aramaic do not distinguish between neuter and masculine and 'the evil' is comfortably ambiguous. Even classical Greek knows *ponēros* in the sense of objectively negative experience (Thuc. 8.97). It is here the same 'evil' from which we pray for protection (Matthew 6.13). *Hārā'a* (*ponēron*: Isaiah 5.20; Amos 5.14; Deuteronomy 13.5; cf. Deuteronomy 4.25 etc.; 17.7, 12, etc.; Proverbs 20.8) is the 'evil' that God inflicts (1 Kings 14.10; 2 Kings 21.12; Jeremiah 26.19; Amos 9.4, etc.). We must not be squeamish in accepting that God inflicts what we please to call 'evil', and we dare not impute an evil purpose to him notwithstanding this. One should not oppose physical or mental affliction,[35] for God himself suffers with his people.[36] The context is *vengeance*, a response to an attack from without. The contrast between the small cohesive community of brethren within and the vast sinful populace without looms large in the background to the antitheses, and must not be lost sight of. The parallel antithesis at 5.43–8 emphasizes, by way both of summary and of climax, that God is the model. Imitating God, whose sun shines on the just and the unjust, and who is perfect, one can seek perfection by loving those who cannot reward one, or are not disposed to do so, in short one behaves, like David *vis-à-vis* Saul, meritoriously (1 Samuel 26.24–5). God cannot acquire merit, but by imitating him one can acquire *standing*, *innocency* in his eyes.

'Eye for an eye . . . ' occurs at Leviticus 24.20 (cf. Exodus 21.23–5; Deuteronomy 19.21), an amelioration of barbarous ways, fitted to the ubiquitous principle 'reward according to deserts' (Leviticus 24.19). It was fair that injuries should not be compensated for beyond their limit, if that could be estimated.[37] Yahweh promised to reward offenders according to their works (Isaiah 3.10–11; Jeremiah 32.19; Romans 2.6). Precise retaliation by God was familiar as a notion in the first century and afterwards.[38] Vengeance is God's alone: it can be indirect, affecting subsequent generations, it can be delayed as in the cases of Ahab and Jezebel, or it can be easily traceable as in the case of David's bastard. Affliction can be diagnosed as divine vengeance, and one must not resist it.

To encourage or allow people to offend is quite another matter. That is itself a sin within Leviticus 19.14, 16, with which Jesus' teaching accords (Mark 9.42 par.; Matthew 18.7; cf. Romans 14.13, 21). But Matthew 5.39b looks very different if one observes that Hosea 11.4 is being quoted. Yahweh treated Israel like an animal, leniently, eased his yoke (Matthew 11.29–30), enabled him to 'feed'. The burden is the divine yoke, the burdens placed upon Israel by Yahweh's stern but loving care, and his concern that they should not be too heavy – a care to which, alas, Israel did not respond. An ancient variant reading (not explicable simply as a confusion of the one changed consonant) is reflected in the Septuagint, but not adopted by the revisers of the same nor by the Masoretes. It was justified as offering a word for word parallel with Isaiah 50.6.[39] The faithful follower is struck on the cheek or jaw, wounded by having the hair pulled out, insulted and hurt; this, however, only enables him to atone for sins. The insult to Yahweh's servant is ascribed to him as merit, for it is proof of God's love for the sinner, in line with the dynamic aspect of Lamentations. Since the word is 'jaws' in the plural, the sufferer turns the other cheek! The reading followed by the Septuagint, remarkable as it is, was regarded as inspired in the first century, and was available to preachers even though not consecrated meanwhile as the standard reading.

Next, Matthew 5.40 speaks of what may be a lawsuit, in which the plaintiff expects to obtain the defendant's shirt (a fine garment). One is expected voluntarily to surrender even the tunic (or cloak) which was protected by the Deuteronomic legislation (Deuteronomy 24.12–13; cf. Exodus 22.26–7), here waived in favour of God's discipline. The plaintiff may be a creditor. This is exactly God's position. Sins are debts (Matthew 5.25–6; 6.12, 14–15; 18.35; Luke 11.4; 13.1–5). Yahweh litigates (Deuteronomy 32.35–6; Psalms 143.2; Micah 6.1–2; cf. Romans 12.19–21; Hebrews 10.29–31), and indeed he does so in the same passage (Isaiah 3.13–15) where the possessor of an outer garment appears superior to all destitute brethren (Isaiah 3.6). There Yahweh threatens those who have been insolent in riches, that he will strip them of every garment, shirts and all (Isaiah 3.16, 24). One must welcome the affliction – becoming aligned towards God. Any human creditor, however unfeeling, in reality is God's deputy. Do not resist him. The Messiah is struck on the cheek and stripped of his garment: the formula is then, for Christians, conclusively authenticated.

The third situation envisaged is that of a taskmaster who impresses one to bear a load for him. It is not a question of politely escorting him. *Angareuein* is a technical expression. It belongs to the transportation-system,[40] with the Hebrew *sbl* (corvée) behind it (1 Samuel 8.11; 2 Chronicles 2.18). He who has the upper hand makes his subordinates carry his bags. A reasonable impresser requires only one mile (he can use relays): the Christian must not hesitate to go two if required. He is not to resent the role of a beast of burden. The 'rights' of the *ad hoc* superiors must be accepted as an article of the divine vengeance. One has no counterclaims against God. One must welcome the impresser (cf. Isaiah 9.4; 14.25) or God's plan is frustrated. For God himself bears patiently and sustains not only Israel (Deuteronomy 32.11; Isaiah 63.9; Hosea 11.3) but the world, through thick and thin (Isaiah 46.4). He sets the example of forbearance. Moses too, as it were, carried Israel interminably. God bears cheerfully the burdens (*sbl*) of others in vicarious suffering (Isaiah 53.4, 11; Lamentations 5.7). By taking the burden of an oppressor one imitates the divine patience, and brings nearer redemption from 'Egypt' (cf. Exodus 1.11, etc.). He who imposes the burden will also remove it, for the Messiah is the means whereby burdens are released (Isaiah 10.27). Bearing the burden willingly one perhaps converts it into an honour (Matthew 3.11), or a load of merit (b. Ber. 17a)!

The fourth situation divides itself into halves (Matthew 5.42). One must give to one who demands, and from an applicant for a loan one must not turn away. True it is, to give to every asker is to court impoverishment, in spite of Psalm 37.25. The text refers, rather, to demands such as that of David at Nob or of Elijah upon the Widow of Zarephath. Moreover, Yahweh promised that Israel would suffer exactions (Isaiah 3.12 LXX). Exactors were to be expected. Jews would have to borrow to pay them (Nehemiah 5.4). Lamentations makes this clear (Lamentations 5.4). One must not evade importunate claims. Of course one should not encourage any brother, who would listen to reason, to fleece his brother; though one of God's creatures' loss is another's gain!

What then of the obligatory 'loan'? From which would-be borrowers would one prefer (left to oneself) to turn away? Surely those who have no security and have small prospects of being able to repay even without interest. Such were the businessmen whom Job subsidized (Test. Iobi 11). Loans without interest were especially meritorious (Deuteronomy 23.19); lending to those who were without security even more so (Deuteronomy 15.8; Psalms 37.26; 112.5; Proverbs 19.17) especially where repayment was doubtful (Psalm 37.21 MT, LXX). It does not appear that Matthew 5.42b simply, and innocuously, reinforces a precept (Leviticus 25.35) to lend to the unsuccessful: something much more significant lies behind the idea. Jesus never turned away, though invited by his disciples often enough to do so. And he provided, by his sacrifice, an infinity of merit to release his followers from bankruptcy (Matthew 20.28). God himself thus continually gives credit to bad risks. He lends, as does the earth itself, continually to man without interest.[41] Deuteronomy 6.10–15 and 8.7–20 exemplify this. His mercy and loving-kindness are shown especially to the undeserving, from whom he will not turn away (Psalms 27.9; 30.7; 31.16; 44.24; 66.19; 69.17 (LXX 68.18); 88.14, etc.; cf. Psalm 22.24). Him one should imitate while one can.

For it is a sign of the divine anger if one *cannot* make a loan, much as one might wish to do so (Deuteronomy 15.6, 8, 10; 24.11; 28.12, 44). In the Age of Wrath Jews will try to borrow, they cannot lend. Foreigners alone will have credit. The importunate beggars will appear as at Isaiah 3.6–7; 4.1. Isaiah 3 has evidently figured largely in the original of this passage. It is a sign of divine favour to be able to lend. Transpose this into the first-century situation. Even to be *presumed* inferior is galling. Social change and subjection to foreign power would increase resentment beyond the point of tolerance. Yet one must not hesitate to pay tax-gatherers, and one must be *glad to lend*, whenever the chance to do so arises. The chance of acquiring merit outweighs the probability of financial loss. So Matthew 5.38–42 deals with the afflictions which amount to four types of aggression: attacks on the person and the honour, attacks on property rights, attacks on liberty,[42] and finally attacks on the credit-worthiness – for one who makes gifts and interest-free loans and loans without security will soon lack credit himself.

So we are quite able to explain Matthew 5.39, *Resist not evil.* 'Evil' is affliction. One must not oppose it, provided it is a misfortune which one is at liberty to choose to internalize, absorb, accept, or, on the contrary, reject and resist. As Lamentations suggests, one must receive the divine vengeance as victim, not institute it. One must be 'pursued', one must not be a 'pursuer'.

Vengeance is God's, requital is his, repayment is his! A cheek-striker, pitiless creditor, impressing soldier or civil-servant, tax-gatherer or customs-officer, or even a destitute fellow-Jew, impose sufferings, but they are sent by God. They may even operate as *tests*.

One of the curiosities of this theory, which the Bible demonstrates quite unselfconsciously, is that Yahweh's instruments of vengeance are identical with the seven nations, or their like, and with Jews infected with the abominations. The acts of oppression under which Jewry is brought to destitution could be done only by such as ignored the Noachide laws! God utilizes abominations to humble, and perfect, his children. They are the rod of his discipline and must be recognized as such. The oppressors will, in their turn, feel the weight of God's vengeance upon *them* (Lamentations 3.64–6, etc.); and if for no other reason the victims must not resist oppression. This is an oriental logic and explains the otherwise unintelligible Mark 14.21 par.

Western man, suspecting that this is nonsense, cannot imagine the deity to have such perverse notions! In reality (as the antitheses show, when decoded) violence (nowhere reprobated as an evil *per se*) is permitted when sanctioned or required by God. But one must not resist, even mentally, a set-back which is part of God's requital of the people's persistent disobedience, especially when he has provided, himself (cf. Genesis 22.8), the means whereby the burdens may be carried, and the debts paid. Needless to say a people's physical defence, against rational human adversaries who can be deterred, by one course or another, from committing sins in the nature of abominations (Leviticus 19.14, 16),[43] is quite another matter, and is not contemplated by Matthew 5.38–42.[44]

Crosses and Cheeks

The cross is taken up deliberately to discipline the body and subdue it (cf. 1 Corinthians 9.27). In addition to this the Lord loves him whom he takes the initiative to chastise (Hebrews 12.5–11). If one takes up a cross, the very sources of sin and also occasions for chastisement are diminished: they are not eliminated because, in that culture, one can be chastised for one's forebear's sins. Accepting lighter sufferings cheerfully, however, one can accumulate merit, and, conceivably, even exonerate others.

One assumes the cross appropriate to one's situation. One

prepares, in this way, for the coming of the Kingdom, since only when unregenerate passions have been tamed can sins be atoned for. Job's self-humiliation in the face of suffering served to atone for the errors of his so-called comforters (Job 42.6–10). To such heroes only is the Land promised.

In a world of clashing ethnicities the idea that one could negotiate with foreigners, or indeed with dissident elements in one's own nation, and so control their conduct by freely stipulated arrangements and bargains, must have seemed hopelessly optimistic and unreasonable. Indeed that is the point of the story of the Gibeonites (Joshua 9). Those who will scruple to swear even by their own gods have little security to fall back upon. One suffered the foreigner and the unscrupulous neighbour much as one suffered the weather; and to suggest that the latter was manipulated by a deity (Amos 4.7) who was arbitrary and unpredictable would be regarded as unhelpful (Psalm 119.68). Man seeks to submit all things to his reason, and here we have part of the reasoning of Asiatic man in his adolescence. Teachers of greater sophistication are still compelled, in this tradition, to use the archaic metaphors, and it seems partly in irony that Matthew chose to make the precepts of Jesus a contrast with the revelations Yahweh made to the ancients.

In each case, it will be found, the revelation through Moses revealed Yahweh's character incompletely since the latter could be checked from elsewhere in Scripture, Scripture equally holy. Yahweh's 'behaviour' glosses the Torah. Jesus, in his time, revealed God's true nature; he expounded his ultimate requirements, and himself satisfied them. What was adequate for the antiquated clients of Moses was not false; it provided a viable idiom which, if properly exploited, would convey a yet further truth. Meanwhile the metaphors of self-amputation, and cross-carrying, which, as we have seen, can speak to the first-century world, Jewish and pagan, are the more viable for their quaint Old Testament pedigree.

It remains to recall that 'taking the cross' has declined in power even during the transmission from the Marcan form to the form we presume existed in Q. The latter isolated the aspect of worthiness.[45] Irrespective of Q's age, Mark preserved a less compromised formulation. The follower of Christ carries that cross irrespective of the opinion of any Church. Whether and how he will have to use it is secret, personal to himself. The Church's intervention, establishing his merit, is irrelevant and an impertinence. I may be allowed to comment that by the time lovers of observances, e.g. fasts, have followed such expression as Paul has ventilated ('I pommel my body and subdue it . . .') in a sense favourable to themselves, Christians have begun to open their ranks to characters little differing from that acceptable to earnest Pharisees.[46]

NOTES

1 As perceived by W. Lüthi and R. Brunner, *The Sermon on the Mount* (Edinburgh and London, 1963), p. 72. The 'cross' saying was studied (*inter alios*) by H. Grotius, *ad* Matthew 10.38, W. Wrede, *Das Messiasgeheimnis in den Evangelien* (Göttingen 1901), p. 138 (Mark 8.34 fits disciples only); G. Dalman, *Jesus–Jeschua* (Leipzig 1922), p. 172; R. Koolmeister, 'Selbstverleugnung', in *Fest. I. Kõpp* (Holmiae 1954), pp. 64–94; E. Dinkler, 'Jesu Wort vom Kreuztragen', in *Fest. R. Bultmann* (*BZNW* 21, Berlin 1954) (an idea not entirely acceptable, since the X-shaped *taw* is extremely archaic); E. Haenchen at *NT* 6 (1963), pp. 81–109 (martyrdom), (so I. H. Marshall, *Luke*, Exeter 1978, p. 373); H. D. Betz, *Nachfolge und Nachahmung Jesu Christi* (Tübingen 1967), p. 30 (risk), (Betz denies that following God figures in the New Testament, but J. M. Nielen had rightly insisted upon it in 1938); K.-G. Reploh, *Markus* (Stuttgart 1969), pp. 123–40; J. G. Griffiths at *NTS* 16 (1970), pp. 358–64 (puzzlement); N. J. McEleney at *CBQ* 34 (1972), pp. 431–60 at 434–5, 442; J. Gnilka, *Markus* II (Zürich, etc., 1979), pp. 22–4. Resisting evil is handled by D. Daube at *JTS* 45 (1944), pp. 177–87; S. C. Currie at *HTR* 57 (1964), pp. 140–5 (do not protest at the wrongdoer); H. Clavier at *RHPR* 1957, pp. 44–57 (Christ is ironical), (Clavier rightly takes *ponērô* as neuter and considers Isaiah 50.5–7; Lamentations 3.30–2; H.-T. Wrege, *Die Überlieferungsgeschichte der Bergpredigt* (Tübingen 1968), pp. 75–82 (the Kingdom is the goal); G. Eichholz, *Auslegung der Bergpredigt* (Neukirchener Verlag 1970²), pp. 92–8 (unreasonable expectations); D. Lührmann at *ZTK* 69 (1972), pp. 412–38. That 'resist not evil' was no insertion of Matthew's (it could be his generalization from the traditional particulars) was the idea of M. J. Suggs, *Wisdom, Christology and Law* (Cambridge, Mass. 1970), p. 110.

2 Josephus, *Ant.* 4.202.

3 For the Middle English uses of 'cross' see the *Shorter Oxford English Dictionary*, s.v. John Wesley wrote (1775) to ask his correspondent to 'take up a cross for him', namely writing to a colleague to whom he did not care to write (again) for himself! The very cheerful hymn, 'Take up thy Cross' (H. A. & M., rev. edn 1950, no. 333), C. W. Everest's adaptation from *Geistliche Gesänge*, 1650, suggests nothing

less likely than a march to crucifixion, rather a defiance of obstacles.

4 *Synopse*[13].

5 G. Dautzenberg, *Sein Leben bewahren* (*SANT* 14), Munich 1966. Jesus' values relate to this life: J. Löfberg, *Spiritual or Human Value?* (Lund 1982), p. 121 *et passim*.

6 Josephus, *B.J.* 2.150.

7 V. C. Pfitzner, *Paul and the Agon Motif* (*Supp. NT* 16), Leiden 1967.

8 Except for radical Christians. L. Tolstoy, *The Kingdom of God is Within You* [1893] (Oxford, World's Classics, 445, 1936/1974), pp. 3–77, utters telling sarcasms, and Aylmer Maude (his biographer) who knew Tolstoy well, and failed to persuade him with his own (justified) doubts concerning Matthew 5.38–42, says (ibid. Introduction, p. x), 'It is curious to note that these words of Christ's had not attracted much scorn or denunciation as long as they slumbered in the obscurity to which they were relegated by the prominence the Church gave to Creeds unrelated to conduct. But as soon as Tolstoy began to repeat them and apply them to real life, the precept attracted both scorn and denunciation. He was himself excommunicated by the Most Holy Synod, placed under police supervision, and had many of his works suppressed by the censor. Dean Farrar referred scornfully to the words as a "divine paradox".' More modern attacks on the precept appear in, for example, G. Friedlander, *Jewish Sources of the Sermon on the Mount* (London 1911), pp. 65–9 (an attack on C. G. Montefiore); A. Plummer, *Matthew* (London 1909), p. 86; A. M. Rihbany, *The Syrian Christ* (London 1919), p. 88; E. Sutcliffe at *Scripture* 51 (1953), pp. 33–5; E. Schweizer, *Matthew* (London 1978), *ad loc.* (do these rules evade involvement, dialogue and exchange? [p. 205]). But the conclusion of J. Wood, *Sermon on the Mount* (London 1963), pp. 98–9 is sound (real reason not noticed).

9 Cf. the correct approach at Ps. Athan. *de pass. et cruce dom.* 6 (PG 28.193 A–C).

10 Derrett at *Bibl.* 63 (1982), pp. 474–505, particularly pp. 499–504; id. at *Hey. J.* 24 (1983), pp. 253–65; id. at *Bibl.* 65 (1984), pp. 168–88; id., at *Downside R.* no. 346, January 1984, pp. 12–21.

11 J. W. Doeve, *Jewish Hermeneutics in the Synoptic Gospels and Acts* (Assen 1953) was badly handled by J. Jeremias, *TLZ* 80 (1955), col. 211 and by J. Dupont, *Béatitudes*, rev. edn (Bruges-Louvain 1958), p. 146 n. 1, apropos of Leviticus 18 and the Sermon on the Mount. The latter frankly acknowledged that if Doeve's theory were right a most valuable research tool had been recovered.

12 C. F. Evans, in D. E. Nineham, ed., *Studies in the Gospels* (Oxford 1955), pp. 37–53, showed Luke's general comparability with Deuteronomy in the central section. This has been scouted by C. L. Blomberg in R. T. France and D. Wenham, eds., *Gospel Perspectives*, III (Sheffield 1980), pp. 212–61 at p. 223. But the nature and purpose of the technique discovered was understood by neither.

13 Derrett, *Studies in the New Testament* III (Leiden 1982), p. 122. Bertram is excellent at *TWNT* 3, pp. 916–17.

14 D. R. A. Hare, *The Theme of Jewish Persecution of Christians in the Gospel according to St Matthew* (SNTS Mon. 6) (Cambridge 1967).

15 Galatians 6.13. A. Satake, in an important study at *ZNW* 67 (1976), pp. 4–19, places such sayings in the thought-world of an apocalyptically-stamped circle. I much prefer the inference to be drawn from the famous phrase at Plato, *Republic* 2.5 (361E–362A), which is on the point. The Daniel haggada used by Mark (Derrett at *Downside Review*, January 1982) suggests that his contemporaries saw that the true Israel was, from the time of Christ, persecuted by *pagans*.

16 At *JBL* 96 (1977), pp. 85–99. See also J. A. Fitzmyer, 'Crucifixion in ancient Palestine . . . ' *CBQ* 40 (1978), pp. 499ff; J. M. Ford at *Expository Times* 87 (1975/6), pp. 275ff; E. Bammel at E. Bammel and C. F. D. Moule, eds, *Jesus and the Politics of His Day* (Cambridge 1984), pp. 441–2.

17 See Theodoret *ad loc.*

18 Derrett at *Revue de Qumran* 11 (no. 43) (1983), pp. 409–15.

19 See, on Genesis 13.13; 14.2, 8, L. Ginzberg, *Legends of the Jews* I, 230. Midrash haggadol I.215–21 (Ginzberg, I, 223 n. 84). The five cities of Sodom, Amorah, Admah, Zeboim and Zoar figure in the Targum ps. Jonathan at Genesis 14.2, 8; 18.24. On the sins of Sodom: J. Bowker, *The Targums and Rabbinic Literature* (Cambridge 1969), pp. 190–2. The men of Sodom broke five out of the seven Noachide commandments (Gen. 13.13 Targum ps. Jonathan).

20 Sight, hearing, taste, touch, smell. Philo, de plant. 133; de cherub. 73; de confus. ling. 52, 90; de mundi op. 117; Test. Naph. 2.8; Sir. 17.5. R. H. Charles, *Apocrypha & Pseudepigrapha* on Test. Reub. ii.3—iii.2. Ps. Plut., de plac. philos. 4.4. Ibn Paquda, *Duties of the Heart* (Jerusalem and New York 1970), I, pp. 111, 115. See lexica for *pentaphōtos*. The dangers of the five senses and the desirability of sacrificing a passion (Exodus 32.27–9) are actually stated by Philo at de ebr. 69–70, cf. de fug. 91. Borgen at NTS 23 (1976), p. 67.

21 Derrett, *Studies in the New Testament* (Leiden 1977), pp. 4–31.

22 554 A–B. See Chariton, *Chaer. et Call.* 4.2.7.

23 Derrett, *The Making of Mark* (Shipston-on-Stour 1985), pp. 147–9.

24 E. Bammel and C. F. D. Moule, eds, *Jesus and the Politics of his Day*. Cambridge 1984.

25 Origen, in Gen. hom. 16.6; in Num. hom. 5.2; and especially 25.3. A. Jaubert, *Origène. Homélies sur Joshué* (*Sources Chrétiennes* 71, Paris 1960), pp. 288–9.

26 Jerome, cont. Iovinianum 1.21 (PL 23, 239–40).

27 Cornelius à Lapide *ad* Jo. 10.22–7 cites Deuteronomy 33.29 rightly. He relates Josh. 8.29 to Colossians 2.14–15; Galatians 6.14. Anon., *The Gospel in the Book of Joshua* (London 1869), pp. 75–6. Gulielmus

Durandus (Durantis), *Rationale divinorum officiorum* (Venice 1549 or Naples 1859) I, 7 ('of the consecration of altars') (tr. J. M. Neale, Leeds 1843, 29, 34) (*gr.* P. Drinkwater).

28 *A New Dial* (no. 64 in *Oxford Book of Carols*, Oxford, 1965), verse 5: 'What are they that are but five?/Five Senses, like five kings, maintain/in every man a several reign.' I owe this also to Mr P. Drinkwater.

29 Halle, 1720, *ad* Josh. 10.19.

30 E. Levine, ed., tr., *The Aramaic Version of Lamentations* (New York 1976). A. van der Heide, *The Yemenite Tradition of the Targum of Lamentations* (Leiden 1981). Martyrdom and suffering for God earns bliss hereafter: Ibn Paquda, op. cit., I, 323, 357–9. Acceptance of misfortunes has atoning power, ib. 317.

31 So expressly the Torah: Numbers 14.33, upon which Isaiah 53 might be based. E. P. Sanders, 'R. Akiba's view of suffering,' *JQR* 63 (1973), pp. 332–51, especially pp. 346–7. 1 Maccabees 2.37. The martyrs of 2 Maccabees and 4 Maccabees are quite explicit. Mekilta, Nez. 18 (Lauterbach III.142). Bab. Talm. Ber. 61b. A. Büchler, *Types of Jewish-Palestinian Piety* (London 1922), pp. 111–14. E. E. Urbach, *The Sages* (Jerusalem 1975) I, pp. 367, 389, 391.

32 Crucifixion: the Lucianic (and possibly very ancient) reading at Lamentations 5.13; Tg. Lam. likewise (see note of Levine, op. cit., pp. 188–9). On the verse and its aftermath see W. Horbury at W. Horbury and B. McNeil, eds., *Suffering and Martyrdom in the New Testament* (Cambridge 1981), p. 154. On trees walking see the study at Derrett, *Studies in the New Testament* III (Leiden 1982), pp. 107–29, but also take account of the fact that opposite to Mark 8.22–6 in the 'grid' must appear Josh. 10.5, 16–27. The transfiguration must be preached against Josh. 10.12–14, and the demonized boy against Josh. 13.2, 6, 13; 14.10.

33 Romans 6.6–11; Galatians 5.24; 6.14 (seen by McEleney, *CBQ* 34, 1972, p. 434). Cf. Galatians 2.19–20; Titus 2.12; Ignat. Rom. 7.7; Iren. Haer. 4.5.4 (PG 7.985C); Orig., comm. in Matthew 12 (PG 13.1037); Greg. Naz., carm. 2.2.20 (PG 1479A); Martyrium Ignatii Colvertinum 2 (O. v. Gebhard, A. Harnack, Th. Zahn. eds., *Patrum Apostolicorum Opera* 2, 1876, pp. 303, 1ff.). 2 Corinthians 4.10 calls for a *nekrōsis*. For Galatians 3.13 see *TWNT* III, pp. 916–17.

34 Romans 6.6–22; 8.3.

35 Affliction. Moffatt's translation was 'injury'. 'Assailant' (Archer, at *Expository Times* 42, 1930–1, pp. 190–1), is too narrow. See Isaiah 3.11 LXX. Our passage has nothing to do with returning evil for evil.

36 P. Kuhn, *Gottes Trauer und Klage in der rabbinischen Überlieferung* (*Talmud und Midrasch*) (*AGAJU* 13) (Leiden 1978).

37 Josephus, *Ant.* 4.280.

38 Judges 1.6–7. Mishnah, Avot II.6. W. Bousset–H. Gressmann, *Die*

Religion des Judentums im späthellistischen Zeitalter (Tübingen 1966[4]), pp. 411–12. Mark 9.42!

39 The LXX (*rapizōn . . . epi tas siagonas autou*) has read *MRṬYM 'L LḤYW* instead of the MT reading *MRYMY 'L 'L LḤYHM*. All correctors of the LXX abandon its reading. *Ṭ* and medial *M* cannot be confused in the scripts of the centuries immediately before Christ. J. Zielger, *Duodecim prophetae* (Göttingen 1943), p. 172, for the evidence.

40 Derrett, *Studies*, III, pp. 165–83.

41 Ex. R. xxxi.

42 H. Grotius *ad* Matthew 5.41 (*Annotationes in Libros Novi Testamenti*, Amsterdam 1641, p. 129).

43 Cf. M. Sanh. 8.7.

44 Violence is of course contemplated at Matthew 24.43/Luke 12.39. See A. Smitmans, 'Das Gleichnis vom Dieb,' *Fest. Schelkle* (Düsseldorf 1973), pp. 43–68.

45 Therefore I hesitate to follow the conclusions of J. Lambrecht, 'Q-influence on Mark 8.34—9.1,' in *Logia. Mémoire J. Coppens* (*BETL* 59) (Leuven 1982), pp. 277–304 (Q the exclusive source).

46 The question whether self-imposed suffering was a cross and redemptive in character was naturally considered by professional ascetics in a region where, as in Buddhist Asia, the public attributed merit to monks. I call to mind the Syriac work surviving in Sogdian (presumably eighth-century) as translated by N. Sims-Williams at *Orientalia Christiana Periodica* 47 (1981), pp. 444–6.

5

Forty Strokes Save One: Social Aspects of Judaizing and Apostasy

A. E. HARVEY

It is now nearly a century since we were warned by Albert Schweitzer that when we seek to establish the lineaments of the historical Jesus we may be doing no more than reading into the Gospels the thoughts and character of our own epoch.[1] In the field of gospel criticism this warning has been largely taken to heart. But a similar danger, which lurks in the study of the epistles and of the history of the early Church, has been less widely noticed. This is the danger of reading back into our understanding of primitive Christianity concepts of religion and religious affiliation which belong to the liberal and pluralist societies of the West, and which may not be appropriate to the ancient world in general and to ancient Judaism and its sects (of which Christianity was originally one) in particular. Commentators on Hebrews, for example, speak of the danger the Christians were exposed to of 'slipping back'[2] or 'returning'[3] into Judaism. Commentators on Matthew speak of the Church having 'split'[4] from the syngaogue, of the evangelist (or Jesus) having various 'attitudes' to the Law under which the synagogue lived.[5] Commentators on Galatians speak of 'Judaizing propaganda'.[6] But was the Jewish community really one you could slip in and out of like a parish church of today? Was the 'pressure to Judaize' really like the pressure exerted by a Jehovah's Witness who has a foot in your door? Even today, the ethnic religious communities of the Middle East are much more rigidly defined than this. They are certainly not such that a Muslim can make an experimental trial of Christianity in the way that an Englishman may try going to church for a while, or that a Jew could go for a period flouting all his Jewish traditions and affiliations and then expect to be received back, without penalties, into the fold. As for the New Testament, the evidence suggests a quite different framework of religious allegiance. When this is understood, a number of texts can be interpreted with a degree of precision which was not available so long as we were working with the western liberal model.

Let us begin by looking at a typical Jewish community in the diaspora (which is where, after all, the vast majority of Jews lived in the ancient world). Its membership consisted almost entirely of persons who were Jewish by birth; but there was also a certain number (how large is a matter of continuing debate) of non-Jewish members who had become proselytes through circumcision and accepted thereby all the responsibilities (Galatians 5.3; Yeb. 47a), though they did not receive quite all the privileges,[7] of membership. This community enjoyed exemption from certain civic duties imposed by the Romans on subject peoples in the Empire. In order that they might observe the sabbath they were excused military service and attendance at civil courts and offices on the sabbath. They were also permitted to arrange their affairs and settle disputes in their own courts.[8] But a necessary consequence of these privileges was that the Jewish community had to maintain a tight discipline within itself. The distinctive features of the Jewish way of life – sabbath observance, keeping of festivals, food taboos and regulations concerning social intercourse with Gentiles – were enforced by their own law, and transgressions against them were punishable by a synagogue court.[9] There is nothing theoretical about the statement that Jews observed the Law of Moses. Any offence under that law made the offender liable to trial and appropriate sentence.

Now it is important to notice that (at least in the diaspora) the jurisdiction of a Jewish court extended only so far as it was willingly accepted. So long as you wanted to stay as a member of the Jewish community, you had no choice but to submit to it. But if for any reason you wished to leave it, it would have no further purchase on you. An example will make this clear. In a city such as Sardis in the first century of our era there is little doubt that the Jewish community possessed a synagogue (the predecessor of the imposing one they acquired in the third century) and that its members were well established in city life.[10] Suppose now that one of their number had the sale of a carpet to negotiate with a Gentile, and was required to bring it for the purpose to the purchaser's house on the sabbath. He might decide that if he took a back street he would escape notice by his fellow Jews, and that for the sake of completing the sale the risk was worth taking. Unfortunately he was spotted! A well-respected Jew challenged him for carrying a burden on the sabbath, another witness appeared, and in the normal way he would have had no option but to appear before the synagogue court so that, after paying the appropriate penalty, he could be reinstated in the community. But (theoretically at least) another option was open to him. He might decide that his carpet business with Gentile customers was of more value to him than his membership of the Jewish community, in which case he could snap his fingers at his accusers. If he did not intend to enter the synagogue again, or to take any further advantage of the rights of membership of the Jewish community, he could simply continue to his destination carrying his carpet. Having renounced the privileges of being a Jew, he had no need to submit to the jurisdiction of any Jewish court. The converse, of course, was also true. If, as a non-Jew, you wished to join the Jewish community, you would be bound to take on its lifestyle and submit to its jurisdiction. It was certainly the case as St Paul says (Galatians 5.3) that everyone who gets himself circumcised is bound to keep the whole law.[11] As a Talmudic saying has it,[12] 'the proselyte is informed of the punishments for the transgression of these precepts'. For, as Josephus reminds us,[13] ignorance of the law was never admitted as a defence in court.

Other relationships with the Jewish community were of course possible. We read in the New Testament of Roman centurions who subscribed to the funds of local synagogues, and whether or not there ever existed an actual class of 'god-fearers'[14] there is no doubt that many Gentiles had intimate contact with Jewish institutions.[15] But there could never be any doubt about who belonged and who did not. Either you conformed to the Jewish way of life, and submitted to the jurisdiction of the Jewish courts, or you were as one of the Gentiles. Movement in and out, therefore, can have been neither casual nor frequent. Gentiles were deterred from joining by what they doubtless regarded as the distasteful Semitic rite of circumcision;[16] and a Jew who left his community forfeited the rights he enjoyed within it and did not necessarily gain corresponding civic rights in the pagan society of which he was now a member.[17] Yet movement undoubtedly did occur. There was the occasional proselyte, the occasional apostate. A notable example is a Jew named Tiberius Alexander, who was procurator of Judaea AD 46–8.[18] As a Roman official he certainly could not conform to the Jewish way of life or submit to the jurisdiction of the Jewish courts. As Josephus says of him, 'he did not abide by his ancestral customs'. At some stage he or his forebears had deliberately broken with the Jewish community. The Law of Moses had no hold over him. Indeed that law did not allow for the act of apostasy: the apostate was by definition removed from its jurisdiction. Only if the apostate wished to return to the fold could it prescribe penalties for offences committed during his apostasy.[19]

In all this, a somewhat special case was posed by the Christians. To an extent which seems to us surprising, new or unorthodox opinions were tolerated within the Jewish community. Difficulties arose only if members of some sect or persuasion failed to conform to the Jewish way of life to the extent of transgressing the law. We may certainly believe the account in the early chapters of Acts (however idealized this may be) according to which the first Christians continued to live and be accepted within the Jewish community: the same situation is presupposed (as we shall see) in Matthew and elsewhere. Indeed in some quarters it may have seemed as if being a Christian made *too little* difference to a Jew. The regulations in the Didache (8.1) that Christians should observe different fast-days from the Jews suggests that Christians felt the need to differentiate themselves by means of distinctive practices which were not actually illegal.[20] And if the usual interpretation of the *birkath-ha-minim* is correct,[21] it presupposes that Christians were continuing to attend synagogues and could not always be easily identified: a shibboleth has no point unless you are not quite sure who are your friends and who your enemies.

Yet it seems that there was also antagonism between Jews and Jewish Christians. Christians suffered, or expected to suffer, judicial penalties at the hands of synagogue courts – which implies both that they wished to remain within the Jewish community (perhaps in some places there was no alternative, short of emigrating) and that they were led by their new faith to commit acts which would seem to justify such penalties. We must look at these matters in more detail later. But in the meantime we can already understand how some Christians could have been asking themselves whether they should continue to identify with the Jewish community, with the risk of being subjected to trial and punishment for offences they were led to commit against the Jewish law, or whether they should definitively separate themselves and 'go into the way of the Gentiles'. Conversely, a church which had separated itself might be under pressure to return. The pressure might come from within, in that the members had come to feel acutely the loss of civic rights and security they had enjoyed in the synagogue. Or if might come from the synagogue, which would naturally not like to be deprived of the support (including financial support) of so many of its former members; and if meanwhile the church had enlisted some Gentiles as members, the question would be bound to arise of subjecting them to circumcision.

Against this background, let us now look at certain New Testament passages which reflect the social and legal aspects of these tensions between Jews and Christians.

'Five times I received forty strokes save one from the Jews' (2 Corinthians 11.24)

Commentators tell us all about the history of this penalty, but quite fail to offer any suggestion how Paul could have incurred it. Had he been living and working within the Jewish community there would have been no problem. The prophecy recorded in Matthew 10.17, 'they shall hand you over to sanhedrins, and they shall flog you in their synagogues', envisages a possibility which may well have become actual for many Jewish Christians.[22] Having decided to remain within the Jewish community, they would have had no option but to submit to the penalties imposed by Jewish courts. But Paul, who before his conversion had never committed an offence (he was 'blameless', Philippians 3.6), had since done his work among Gentiles and set up Christian communities outside the jurisdiction of the synagogue. How then did he come to incur this penalty no less than five times? And what led him to submit to it?

We have first to consider what offence, among those punishable by flogging, could plausibly have been committed by Paul. We must not expect to be able to give a definitive answer to this question. To a certain extent flogging was a discretionary penalty, and could be imposed for a wide variety of offences.[23] In the Mishnah[24] it could take the place of *krt* (exile), which still further broadens the field of crimes for which it might be a punishment; and it could vary greatly in severity according to the seriousness of the offence.[25] Paul however makes it clear that on five occasions he received the maximum penalty, so that we evidently have to do with serious offences. We can safely exclude any charge based on alleged doctrinal heresy, not only because Jewish society was extremely tolerant of deviant opinions and such charges do not seem to have come before the courts, but because it is extremely unlikely that a Jewish court in Paul's time, composed as they normally were of judges of different traditions and affiliations,[26] would have agreed on the verdict (cf. Acts 23.6ff!) This leaves only two charges on which Paul is likely to have been convicted: blasphemy;[27] and serious offences against Jewish customs.[28] Paul says of himself, according to Luke (Acts 26.11), that when he was persecuting the Christians he 'compelled them to blaspheme' in the course of punishing them. This is usually taken to mean[29] that under such harsh treatment the persecuted Christians abjured Christ, and so committed what, from the Christian point of view, must be regarded as blasphemy. But it seems more probable that Paul forced them to say what they really believed about Christ: that this person who had been condemned under the Jewish law was now exalted at God's right hand. This at any rate was Stephen's offence,[30] and Paul had concurred with those who regarded it as punishable by death. After his conversion, it is quite possible that Paul found himself in the same situation, and made professions of faith about Jesus which a Jewish tribunal regarded as blasphemous. But the normal punishment for this was stoning (Leviticus 24.16); and indeed Paul says that he once received it ('once I was stoned', 2 Corinthians 11.25). The surprising thing is that he lived to tell the tale – did a Roman soldier come round the corner just in time? It seems likely therefore that his five floggings were inflicted on him for a slightly less serious offence. The Mishnah mentions[31] profaning the sabbath, working on the Day of Atonement, and a number of offences connected with food and ritual cleanness. These are just the kind of offences Paul would have been liable to commit by his intimate association with Gentile Christians. We can assume with some measure of confidence that they were the cause of his five maximum floggings. But we still have the question, why did Paul submit to them? We may be in a better position to answer when we have looked at some other instances of Jewish jurisdiction and Christian submission.

The Christians at Antioch (Galatians 2.11–21)

This was a predominantly Gentile church, though with some

Jewish Christians among them. They had evidently adopted the practice of meals shared in common: we must assume therefore that the Jews among them had broken with the local synagogue – there is no mention either of being under its jurisdiction or of pressure from that quarter. But a new factor was introduced by the visit of Cephas from Jerusalem. Cephas himself, though still resident in Jerusalem and therefore subject to the synagogue's jurisdiction (how otherwise could a Jew live in Jerusalem?), was prepared to share these common meals during his visit (he 'ate with the Gentiles', 2.12), presumably on the assumption that there was no reason to fear any consequences. But the situation changed when a whole deputation arrived from Jerusalem. Peter then began to absent himself from the common meals, and his example was followed by the other Jewish members of the church. Paul calls this a 'pretence';[32] that is to say, they were 'pretending' to the Jerusalem delegation that they were following the normal Jewish pattern of observance. He also says that Peter adopted this policy 'fearing those of the circumcision' (2.12). What was he afraid of? Their moral disapproval? We must credit Peter with a greater strength of conviction than this. But he could have had real cause for fear in that his intercourse with Gentiles, being illegal according to Jewish Law,[33] could hardly remain unknown in Jerusalem once it had been witnessed by a group of Jerusalem Christians, who had themselves not yet been convinced that such conduct was a necessary consequence of becoming a Christian. Peter might then have faced a charge in a Jerusalem court: he too might have suffered forty strokes save one.

Paul's answer is, first, that moral pretence is indefensible: 'If you, being a Jew, live in a Gentile, not in a Jewish, way' (a reference to Peter's previous table-fellowship) 'how can you compel the Gentiles to adopt Jewish customs?' (which would be the consequence of his change of policy if any table-fellowship was to be preserved: meals would have to be strictly *kosher*, and held in Jewish houses). Secondly, it is theological: The Christian can have no motive for respecting Jewish observances for their own sake, since they cannot give any assurance that one is doing right (2.15–16). But, thirdly, does he not take into view the practical consequences? Peter might have to face a severe flogging. But Paul himself has had the same experience – by the time he wrote Galatians he may well have received at least one of his severe penalties. He has found in it a spiritual experience. Jesus submitted to conviction and sentence under the Jewish law[34] which resulted in his death. He 'handed himself over for me' (2.20). It is open to Jesus' followers to make a similar voluntary submission to legal penalties; it is a way of 'dying to the law through the law', of being 'crucified with Christ' (2.19f). It is only by being ready to face this that one can be sure one is not acting *for the sake* of abiding by the Law. The moment one does that, one has lost touch with Christ. There is then *no point* (for oneself) in his death (2.21).

Christians in Galatia (Galatians 3—4)

We have here what appears to be a unique situation. The church is composed of non-Jews (they are being asked to undergo circumcision); but they are under pressure from the Jewish community to adopt the Jewish way of life. How can this have happened? Theoretically, it is possible that it was a case of straight proselytization. These Gentiles, by becoming Christians, might seem to have come half-way (so to speak) into Judaism. A little more pressure, and they might come the rest of the way. But this would hardly account for the fact that the Christians were actually being subjected to harassment (1.7; 5.10): Paul can even say that they are being 'forced' to be circumcised (6.12). Moreover, he uses language appropriate, not to joining the Jewish community, but to returning to it (4.9). We must therefore assume that this church had been founded along the lines so often described in Acts. Paul had detached from the synagogue a substantial group of Gentile sympathizers – those whom it is customary to describe as 'god-fearers'. The synagogue would naturally view this situation with some bitterness. It had lost the support (doubtless including the financial support[35]) of a number of its former adherents. Moreover the dissident group continued to profess many aspects of the Jewish religion, it revered the same Scriptures and used similar forms of worship. It was 'profaning the Name'. The synagogue would therefore do all it could to bring them back; and this time (it seems) it would make adherence permanent by obliging them to undergo circumcision.

We have no means of knowing what measures were open to the synagogue to bring this about. Their courts had no jurisdiction over those who had left their community (especially if they were Gentiles); and any attempt to put serious pressure on them through social harassment or commercial embargoes would have had the effect of driving them further away into the non-Jewish society of their city. They must therefore have had to content themselves with propaganda and personal persuasion; and indeed it is against this that Paul addresses most of his arguments in the course of his Letter. They seem also to have secured the help of a party within the Christian congregation, who were doubtless able to exert stronger pressure (Galatians 6.13). The temptation for the Christians was of course to think that they could get the best of both worlds. Why should they not rejoin the synagogue, but at the same time continue to meet for Christian worship and fellowship? Paul's answer is mainly concerned to demonstrate the disastrous theological implications of what evidently seemed to the Galatian Christians to be nothing more serious than a convenient practical compromise.[36] But behind the theological argument lies an issue with serious practical consequences. If the Christians rejoined the synagogue – and still more if they became proselytes through circumcision – they would come under the jurisdiction of the Jewish court. If, through their Christian fellowship and social intercourse with non-Jews, they persisted in illegal acts, they must expect to be punished. Perhaps they would even receive forty strokes save one!

Echoes of this practical issue can be heard even in Paul's highly theological argument. The Galatians had already decided to observe Jewish sabbaths and festivals. Many pagans already did this, to the scandal of the more exclusivist Jewish authorities.[37] But in the Galatians' case this was more than the mere adoption of Jewish customs. Paul says, 'You are *observing* days and months and seasons and years' (4.10). The verb (*paratērein*)is significant. One way in which the Jerusalem Sanhedrin maintained its authority over the synagogues of the diaspora was by reserving the right to 'observe' the new moon and to make adjustments to the calendar.[38] In the same way the local synagogue asserted its authority by upholding official decisions over the timing of any sacred season. Anyone who decided seriously to observe these days and seasons was thereby implicitly acknowledging the authority of the synagogue.

But the Christians were also those 'before whose eyes Jesus Christ was placarded as crucified' (3.1). According to the Law of Moses, he was 'accursed' (3.13). It followed that anyone who confessed allegiance to him would be disputing that verdict and denying the absolute authority of the law to determine what conduct was right or wrong. It would therefore be impossible to become a law-abiding member of the community that was bound by that law. One would have to reserve one's right to adopt courses of action which the law forbade. In which case one might find oneself either incurring legal penalties or forced to leave the community.

This is precisely the consequence Paul had undergone. He had submitted to the full penalties which he incurred by his style of life. In 4.13 he reminds the Galatians that when he first preached to them he did so 'through weakness of the flesh'. He then adds the puzzling statement: 'You did not take lightly or show disgust at this your temptation (*peirasmos*) in my flesh.' Translators recognize the difficulty of this sentence,[39] and commentators suggest rather lamely that the Galatians had been 'tempted' to despise Paul because of his apparently enfeebled condition. But what sort of 'temptation' would an illness of Paul's have placed in their way? Suppose however that his 'weakness' was the evident result of a maximum scourging. It would have been clear proof of the danger of holding this new variant of the Jewish religion in close proximity to the Jews. This was the physical side of 'dying to the law' – perhaps indeed it was this that Paul called the *stigmata* of Jesus which he bore in his body (6.17); and the Galatians, who had gained much from their adherence to the synagogue (including their knowledge of Scripture), might well have been 'tempted' to turn away from Paul's message if this was the treatment it had brought upon Paul and could bring upon them if they sought to maintain their ties with the Jews. Conversely, it could be represented that, if the whole Christian congregation were to be circumcised and adopt the Jewish way of life, all danger of incurring penalties through consorting with Gentiles and following their customs would be removed. Christians would then 'make a good showing in the flesh' (6.12), in that they would never be likely to incur such penalties as would show (like Paul's) in their physical appearance.

Hebrews

Here we have a totally different situation from that in Antioch or Galatia, in that the church is entirely Jewish. This can be inferred, not just from the traditional title of the treatise (which may be no more than a reasonable inference from its contents) but from the exhortation in 13.13 to 'come out to him (Jesus) outside the camp, bearing the abuse (*oneidismos*) he endured'. This is clearly a call to the Christians to separate themselves from an existing community and stand on their own feet. And if we ask, to what community in the ancient world is it plausible that these Christians belonged before their conversion, only one answer is possible: that of the Jews. No other communities existed (or none, at any rate, which they are likely to have belonged to[40]) which bound their members in such solidarity that an appeal of this kind to 'come out' of it would have made any sense. These Christians were Jews. And in 10.32–4 we are given some glimpses of the social consequences of their conversion to Christianity.

'Remember the earlier days in which, having been enlightened, you endured a great course of sufferings . . .' Again, we need be in no doubt that these sufferings were inflicted by the Jewish community from which they had separated themselves. They appear to have taken the following forms:

(*a*) insults and harassment on public occasions (*theatrizomenoi*);
(*b*) the anxiety that went with being identified with those who were being publicly persecuted;
(*c*) confiscation of goods. This could, of course, have been simple robbery, and Christians might have been denied the opportunity of redress in the courts. But there was precedent in Ezra 7.26 (cf. 10.8) for judicial confiscation, and there is some evidence that it continued to be used in cases where no specific penalty was provided for the offence;[41]
(*d*) imprisonment. This was not a standard penalty. It was occasionally used for a serious offence when the court was unable to impose the death penalty;[42] but its most common use was in the case of a debtor unable to pay his debt.[43] It would be a natural sequel to the confiscation of goods: the Christian who suffered this would lose all means of credit and be liable to be sued by his creditors and imprisoned when he defaulted.

All this clearly placed the Christians under pressure. Some, it seems, had left the church and joined its persecutors (10.29): a solemn warning has to be given that there can be no readmission if things get easier and they want to return (6.4). Others are tempted to keep a low profile, and even to 'stay away from meetings' (10.25).[44] The author therefore exhorts them to maintain their boldness of speech (*parrhēsia*, 10.35) and devotes much space to inculcating the quality of endurance (*hypomonē*, 12.1–11). For clearly things have reached a point where Christians can no longer coexist peaceably with Jews within the Jewish community. In one sense, there can have been nowhere else for them to go: it must have been extremely difficult in a Hellenistic city for a group of people who were known to be Jews to achieve any civic rights in separation from the Jewish community. Yet in this case it seems they had no option; and once we begin to see the seriousness of their situation we can appreciate why the author had to adopt such an urgent style in exhorting them to remain faithful.

Matthew

The composition of 'Matthew's church' has been the subject of much discussion, and cannot be taken as settled. Certainly the subsequent history of Matthew's Gospel, and its popularity in non-Jewish congregations, shows that it does not have a narrowly Jewish orientation. Nevertheless, such references as there are to the social situation of its readers tell strongly in favour of a uniformly Jewish membership. How otherwise would they have felt comfortable when they were assembled to hear that they should treat a hardened sinner as they would 'a Gentile or a publican' (18.17)? And what weight could they have given to the threat of 'being handed over to Jewish tribunals' (10.17) if a subsantial number of them consisted of non-Jews over whom those tribunals could exercise no jurisdiction? It is reasonable to assume that, at least in its earliest stages, 'Matthew's church' was a Jewish congregation.

In this respect they were like the church which received the Letter to Hebrews. But in other respects they were very different. The 'Hebrews' were being encouraged to leave the synagogue and defy its jurisdiction. The readers and hearers of Matthew's Gospel, by contrast, must continue to respect Rabbinic authority (23.2) and must bring no reproach on the Jewish community through any failure in 'righteousness' by the standards of the Jewish law (5.20). They may be a distinct group with their own discipline and organization: indeed they seem to have thought of themselves as a separate 'synagogue', over against '*their* synagogues', i.e. those of the non-Christian Jews (10.17; 12.9; cf. 23.34). But there is no question of having already deserted the Jewish community or of having placed themselves outside its jurisdiction. Indeed it is only (as we shall see) on the assumption that they remained under that jurisdiction that we can make sense of Jesus' prophecies of their impending persecution; and the *birkath-ha-minim* itself, which is usually thought to mark the final breach between a Jewish church of this kind and the synagogue, in the 'eighties of the first century,[45] presupposes that Christians still gathered for worship in Jewish synagogues.

The gospel read in this church contained specific prophecies of Jewish persecution. 'They shall hand you over to tribunals, and flog you in their synagogues' (10.17). 'I will send you prophets and wise men and scribes: some of them you will kill and crucify, and some you will flog in your synagogues and drive from city to city' (23.34). 'Blessed are you when men revile you and persecute you' (5.11). The reviling and persecuting is reminiscent of the social and unofficial harassment suffered by the 'Hebrews'; 'killing' and 'crucifying' may be deliberate exaggerations in order to bring the destiny of the disciples into line with the (now legendary) deaths of the Old Testament prophets.[46] But 'flogging in synagogues' is unambiguously judicial, a penalty for a specific offence.

What offence were they likely to be charged with? The commentaries maintain a notable silence on this subject, and even the more specialized studies have little to offer beyond speculation.[47] We can get a certain distance towards an answer by a process of elimination. We have observed that the Christians met in their own 'synagogue'; but there can have been nothing illegal in this. We know from Acts of the existence of synagogues for particular classes of Jews (such as freedmen, 6.9) and it has been plausibly suspected that the 'Hellenists' had an approach to Judaism very different from, say, the Pharisees.[48] The fact of separate assembly, therefore, can hardly have amounted to an offence. Nor have we any reason to think that the Christians would break the law with regard to the sabbath or to ritual cleanness: the instructions preserved in the gospel point rather towards a punctilious respect for generally accepted observances. It seems, too, that they were hardly in the situation to give offence by social intercourse with Gentiles. There are in fact only two possibilities. If they publicly used the kind of language about the leaders and elders of the

Jewish community which Jesus had used (according to their gospel) when criticizing the Pharisees, this could well have caused resentment, disorder and a demand for retribution in the synagogue community. Jesus ben Ananias presents an analogous case here. His constant railing against the Temple in Jerusalem was a threat to public order, and the Jewish leaders had him arrested and flogged 'because of his evil speaking'.[49] It is possible that the Christians felt bound to adopt a similarly provocative stance and therefore risked a similar punishment. But it is also possible that we can find a clue in the Beatitude which mentions that Christians would be insulted and persecuted 'for Jesus' sake'. In a sense, of course, any penalty they suffered would ultimately be on account of their religion, and so 'for Jesus' sake'. But the phrase is more pointed if their offence itself arose directly from their distinctive faith. We have seen that in Paul's case it was reasonable to think that the acknowledgement as an exalted Lord of the Jesus who had been properly condemned according to the Jewish law might incur a charge of blasphemy; and that if the offence was regarded as nevertheless not serious enough to warrant the death penalty (or if an execution was for other reasons not practicable) flogging would have been an appropriate penalty. Such a scenario had only to seem a real possibility to Matthew's church (even if it had not been experienced) for them to attend respectfully to Jesus' prophecy: 'they will flog you in their synagogues'.

On this point – the precise nature of the offences the Christians might commit – we can have no certainty. But we still have not addressed ourselves to the fundamental question with which we began: why did they submit to the jurisdiction of the synagogue at all? Why did they not simply remove themselves from the Jewish community, and have no further dealings with its institutions? The answer may be simply that they had nowhere else to go. In a ghetto situation in any town or city it could have been impossible to sustain any social existence at all without belonging to the Jewish community. Short of moving their homes, they may have had no option but to conform. Yet there is a hint in Matthew's Gospel of a more profound reason. These Christians must have heard of the amazing success of evangelistic work among the Gentiles, and of the astonishing growth of non-Jewish churches. In their own Gospel it was recorded that this was according to the will of the risen Christ: 'Go and make disciples of all the nations' (28.19). By contrast, their own mission to their fellow Jews was proving slow and discouraging. How tempting it must have been for them to 'come out of the camp', as other Christians had done; to throw off the jurisdiction of the Jewish authorities, to put an end to the threat of flogging and harassment by the synagogue, and to turn their energies to a task that seemed so much more propitious, the evangelization of the Gentiles. But no, they were recalled to the harder path by words of Jesus which have caused endless trouble to commentators but which they may have found highly relevant to their situation: 'Go not into the way of the Gentiles' (10.5). Their mission was to the house of Israel, and they would by no means have exhausted its possibilities before the Son of Man came (10.23). For this purpose they must remain within the Jewish community even if this meant being exposed to the threat of being 'handed over to their tribunals and flogged in their synagogues'.

This at last is surely the answer to the question from which we started. We have considered the possible offences on account of which Paul could have incurred the extremely severe penalty of forty strokes save one. But why did he submit to it, not once but five times? Like Matthew's church, he needed to maintain his access to the synagogues. Having committed an offence and having been found guilty by Jewish courts, he had to discharge the sentence imposed on him before he could be readmitted to the Jewish community and continue preaching where his missionary work had most effect – among the Gentile sympathizers. Moreover he never abandoned the attempt to convert his fellow Jews; and we can now give full practical and social weight[50] to his own words when he writes, 'I became to the Jews as a Jew, so that I might gain Jews; to those under the law as one under the law (not being myself under the law) so that I might gain those under the law'. Had he remained, like the Christians of Matthew's Gospel, content with a mission to the Jews, his being 'under the law' might have been a painless constraint. But to combine this with being 'as not under the law to those not under the law' – that is, with adopting Gentile customs in open breach of the legal requirements of Jewish society – was to incur the virtual necessity of regular punishment in order to maintain his Jewish connections. It was a heroic course, of a piece with all those other ordeals which Paul underwent for the sake of the gospel. But none of them is likely to have exceeded, in the sheer damage it caused to his physique (let alone the humiliation to his person), the five occasions on which he received from his fellow Jews the maximum judicial penalty of forty strokes save one.

NOTES

1 Cf. *The Quest of the Historical Jesus* (ET London 1910), p. 4: 'Each successive epoch of theology found its own thoughts in Jesus . . . each individual created Him in accordance with his own character.'

2 F. F. Bruce, *Peake's Commentary on the Bible* (London 1962), p. 880e.

3 A. Nairne, *Hebrews* (Cambridge Greek Testament 1917, RP 1957), p. lxxxiv.

4 E. Schweizer, *The Good News according to Matthew* (London 1976), p. 16.

5 W. D. Davies, *The Setting of the Sermon on the Mount* (Cambridge 1964), pp. 425ff.

6 E. de W. Burton, *Galatians* (ICC Edinburgh 1921), p. lv.

7 M. Bik. 1.4; Philo *Spec. Leg.* 1.51f.

8 V. Tcherikover, *Hellenistic Civilization and the Jews* (Philadelphia 1961), pp. 301, 307.

9 J. Juster, *Les Juifs dans l'Empire Romain* (Paris 1914) 1, p. 421; 2, p. 153.

10 A. T. Kraabel in G. M. A. Hanfmann, *Sardis from Prehistoric to Roman Times* (Harvard 1983), p. 179.

11 t.Dem 2.5 (text: Lieberman): 'We do not accept a convert who has accepted upon himself all the laws of the Torah except one' – probably a first-century text, cf. L. H. Schiffman, 'At the Crossroads: Tannaitic Perspectives on the Jewish-Christian Schism', in *Jewish and Christian Self-Definition*, 2 (London 1981), pp.115–56 at p.124 and n. 58.

12 Yeb. 47a.

13 *C.Ap.* 2.178.

14 A. T. Kraabel, 'The Disappearance of the "God-fearers"' *Numen* 28.2 (1981), pp. 113–26, has drawn attention to the total lack of epigraphical evidence, and the ambiguity of the literary evidence, for a class of *sebomenoi* or *phoboumenoi*. But the story of Paul's mission, and indeed of the influence of Judaism on the pagan world generally, would be unintelligible without the existence of *some* half-way stage before becoming a full proselyte. See the discussion in Schürer (as in n. 33) 3 (forthcoming).

15 Josephus, *C.Ap.* 2.282; Tertullian, *Ad Nationes* 1.13.

16 S. Sandmel, *Judaism and Christian Beginnings* (New York 1978), p. 231, surely understates the matter when he writes that circumcision was 'conceivably a deterrent'. For the opposite view (equally unsup-

ported by evidence), that circumcision was regarded as 'barbaric' and 'perverse', see R. Meyer in *TWNT* 6, p. 78.

17 Tcherikover, op.cit., p. 331.

18 Josephus, *Ant.* 20.100.

19 *Enc. Jud.* 1.212, s.v. 'Apostasy', cf. L. H. Schiffman in *Jewish and Christian Self-Definition* 2, p. 146: a discussion of *meshummadim.*

20 Cf. J. P. Audet, *La Didache* (Paris 1958), p. 209.

21 For example, M. D. Goulder, *Midrash and Lection in Matthew* (London 1974), pp. 151–2. But its relevance is still called into question by, for example, R. Kimelman in *Jewish and Christian Self-Definition*, 2, pp. 226–44.

22 Cf. R. Hummel, *Die Auseinandersetzung zwischen Kirche und Judentum im Matthäus-evangelium* (Munich 1963), p. 160.

23 Z. W. Falk, *Introduction to Jewish Law of the Second Commonwealth*, 2 (Leiden 1978), p. 160.

24 M. Makk. 3.15. Cf. A. Hultgren, 'Paul's Pre-Christian Persecution of the Church', *JBL* 95 (1976), p. 104.

25 *Jewish Encyclopaedia* 11.570 s.v. 'Stripes'; cf. *Enc. Jud.* 4.720–1.

26 J. D. M. Derrett, *Studies in the New Testament* 1 (Leiden 1977), pp. 34f; 113f.

27 M. Ker. 1.1 (cf. M. Makk 3.15).

28 M. Makk. 3.2.

29 The great majority of commentators take this for granted, comparing Pliny, *Ep.* 10.96.5, *maledicere Christo.*

30 Acts 7.55–8. So, for example, E. Haenchen, *Die Apostelgeschichte* (Göttingen 1961), *ad loc.*: 'Gotteslästerung'.

31 M. Makk. 3.2.

32 Cf. J. B. Lightfoot, *Galatians* (RP London 1905), *ad loc.*: 'The idea at the root of *hypokrisis* is not a false motive entertained but a false impression produced'.

33 E. Schürer, *History* (ed. Vermes, Millar, Black), 2 (Edinburgh 1979), pp. 83f.

34 I have argued in *Jesus and the Constraints of History* (London 1982), p. 22, that this is what Paul believed.

35 Cf. K. Berger, 'Almosen für Israel', *NTS* 23 (1977), pp. 180ff.

36 Cf. A. Harvey, 'The Opposition to Paul', *Studia Evangelica* 4 (1968), pp. 319–32.

37 Tertullian *Ad Nationes* 1.13; Deuteronomy R.1; Hippolytus *Ref.* 9.21.

38 S. Sandmel, *Judaism and Christian Beginnings*, pp. 209ff.; M. D. Herr in *Compendia Rerum Judaicarum* 2 (Assen/Amsterdam 1976), pp. 843ff.

39 The New English Bible offers two alternative renderings.

40 The suggestion that these Christians had all previously belonged to some mystery religion or other pagan association is extremely improbable.

41 Falk, op.cit., 2, p. 163.

42 Falk, op.cit., 2, p. 162.

43 Matthew 18.30 etc.; cf. J. D. M. Derrett, *Jesus's Audience* (London 1973), p. 65.

44 Cf. M. Aboth 2.5: 'Keep not aloof from the congregation'.

45 See above, n. 21.

46 Cf. H. Fischel, 'Martyr and Prophet', *JQR* 37 (1946), pp. 265–80.

47 D. R. S. Hare, *The Theme of Jewish Persecution in Matthew* (Cambridge 1967), pp. 43–6: 'maintenance of public order'. J. Dupont, *Les Béatitudes*, (Bruges 1958) 2, p. 289: Christians are treated 'comme gens qu'on tient à l'écart'.

48 O. Cullmann, *The Johannine Circle* (ET London 1976), pp. 32f and elsewhere.

49 Josephus *B.J.* 6.302.

50 It is notable that no social and practical implications are taken into account in H. Chadwick's well-known article on this passage, 'All things to all men', *NTS* 1 (1954–5), pp. 261–75. C. K. Barrett, in his Commentary on 2 Corinthians (London 1973) *ad loc.*, comes near to this solution when he writes, 'Paul did not lightly give up his Jewish status and connection'. E. P. Sanders, *Paul, the Law, and the Jewish People* (Philadelphia 1983), p. 192, sees the problem clearly ('had he wished, he could have withdrawn from Jewish society altogether and thus not have been punished'), but offers the solution that Paul submitted to make a *theological* point: 'the question of who constitutes Israel was a matter of crucial importance'.

6

Ears to Hear

F. GERALD DOWNING

I

A small group of Christians in Rome is listening to a lector reading from a brand new scroll. They recognize most of the stories: they've heard them singly, and some of them in short sequences, many times before. They've told them to one another, and know many of them off by heart. But they've never put them all together in a string; and though they've heard the tale of Jesus' arrest and trials and execution frequently, it has never been expanded with so many extra tales. And then it stops, with 'for they were afraid'. The people don't discuss it with one another or with the reader, and Marcus isn't there himself to gauge their response. He's written it to express his belief, his understanding, and they can take it or leave it. He hasn't discussed his project in advance, and he certainly isn't going to change it now, so why talk about it? He only has to hope lots of copies will be made and circulated before anyone else steals this brilliant innovation of his. And so the people take it as it stands. Never having heard any such extended string of incidents read out to them before in their lives, they have no preconceived ways of appraising it. 'This is *sui generis*', they say.

It is a quite implausible picture; but it seems to be presupposed by much otherwise very promising contemporary scholarship. The Gospels have been quarried for information about Jesus, and then for information about the early Christian communities, creating, preserving and adapting the traditions about Jesus; but when we concentrate on the works as such, we are left supposing we are looking only at authors and at an enclosed narrative world which excludes any real audience. An 'ideal audience' may be discerned, but the actual community (and communication within it) may now safely be forgotten (and an 'ideal author' is more convenient than a real one).[1] Where such an artificial construct is openly acknowledged it may enable a very enjoyable appreciation, and even raise pertinent historical questions. Where it is unavowed in a supposedly historical critique it must lead to damaging distortions.[2]

In her recent study of Josephus, Tessa Rajak draws attention to the younger Pliny 'telling us that it was customary for authors to give readings from their productions before invited audiences in order to gather useful criticisms and be able to insert corrections before the final version was issued, and that he went as far as to do the same with his speeches.'[3] Josephus may be assumed to have done the same, and certainly indicates that he submitted his work early to important patrons.[4] Dr Rajak refers us also to Cicero; but we may further compare Quintilian on the 'social' character of publication;[5] and Dio of Prusa.[6] There does not seem to be any first-century model for an author creating a work out of his own undiscussed perceptions for an audience whose response he must simply imagine or note when it is too late to respond.

An author in isolation from his audience appears as a powerful 'authoritative' figure. It is he who selects the message and the medium, however much he may share available media with any audience that may happen upon his work. So a work such as the Gospel of Mark looks to most to be simply Judaeo-Christian (because that is the setting where the events and the stories about them come from); and the message is to be found by discerning the author's intention from emphases and repetitions and collocations and patterns. There are a few concessions to non-Jews (7.3–4, on ritual washing, for instance). But there are no pagan stories, no pagan philosophical catchwords. The only context that seems to demand attention is the Jesus tradition, its Jewish setting – and the mind of the author, as filter, adapting and composing. The 'author' is originator, and origin is all, it is supposed.

Yet if instead we adopt the much more plausible model of the author in constant conversation with his audience, it is at once clear that we have to take the pagan setting (however unsure we may be of it in detail) very much more seriously. The audience, we know (from passages like 7.3–4), is not Jewish; nor is it a second generation that has grown up in an isolated Christian ghetto. The audience is composed mainly of adults who have grown up sharing in the rich popular culture of some Graeco-Roman city, Rome itself, or some other. Even if they cannot all read (though many may be able to), they will have enjoyed a full and varied diet of oral stimulation, from story-tellers, sophists, itinerant philosophers, pleaders in the courts, and local politicians and others at civic assemblies; if not at first hand, then at second or third.

Some of the clearest evidence is in the discourses of Dio of Prusa, repeated in many urban centres, copied (and sold), ranging widely through art, politics, religion, economics, social philosophy, and richly illustrated with stories. The audience for which he was competing is illustrated by his account of Alexandria:

> The city contains no small number of Cynics. Like any other movement, this one has had its crop of persons whose tenets, to be sure, comprise practically nothing spurious or ignoble – yet they must make a living. These Cynics, posting themselves at street-corners, in alley-ways, and at temple gates, pass round the hat and play upon the credulity of lads and sailors and crowds of that sort . . .[7]

Philo paints a very similar picture for the city half a century or so earlier.[8] And Dio seems to have used much the same material in Greece and Asia Minor and Rome. When Quintilian discusses speeches for lay jurists, and for civic occasions, he too seems to presuppose the same kinds of expectation: 'we most often express our views before an ignorant audience (*imperitos*) and more especially before popular assemblies, of which the majority is usually uneducated . . . '[9] If Mark was in any way responsive to his audience, it would be one fully accustomed to narrative as entertainment and as at the same time the communication of ethics, politics and theology.[10]

The only other model that might serve to dispense with the complication of this popular pagan culture would be, as hinted above, that of the author in a ghetto with followers secluded from the world. Though such a model might seem at first sight perhaps to fit at least 'the community of the beloved disciple', Raymond Brown has shown how much more complex a picture is demanded even there; and C. H. Dodd's earlier findings are not to be neglected.[11] For no other New Testament writer can there be found any warrant for such a hypothetical isolation of the author from the pervasive influence of Graeco-Roman culture *in his audience* (however little or much he has himself assimilated).

It is perhaps worth adding that not only is such an implicit or explicit individualist understanding of first-century literary composition unhistorical, but it also suggests a rather strange view of language and communication. In most studies of linguistics 'feedback' to the speaker in any attempt to communicate is accorded prime importance. The response of a hearer forms an integral part of Wittgenstein's analysis of the impossibility of any truly 'private language'. The 'coming to agreement' of speaker and hearer is essential to Jürgen Habermas's 'universal pragmatics', based on J. L. Austin and J. R. Searle, among others.[12] That any of the Gospels could have been composed in author's 'private narrative language' and still have seemed worth preserving is barely conceivable. Even the self-contained romantic author of more recent times, who writes from his own perceptions for an audience which he also creates, writes out of a context at least of past communication; and his *fait accompli* (ignoring publishers and editors) only works if his divination has been correct, and a 'real' readership finds itself in his construction. First-century literary composition must be taken, however, to have been explicitly and actively collaborative. Any attempt to understand the New Testament writings demands a quest for the historical audience; although we must always allow that the demand may not be at all satisfactorily met.

I hope this may have established at least some initial plausibility for this model of first-century literary composition. It is necessary then to attempt some clearer definition of the kind of part likely to have been played by the audience.

In the first place it seems unlikely that an audience would simply want its ideas echoed back (however much it might want its own views reinforced). The fact that New Testament scholarship has been able to concentrate so much on author's contributions shows quite clearly that the *matter* is not provided by the audience's pagan cultural past and present context (or not to any considerable degree), whether or not the author shares that past. The likeliest major contribution of the audience is in terms of selection. The audience lets it be known by its response where its interests lie, and what it can or cannot understand. The author chooses 'from stock' items and patterns to match. An audience appreciates narrative composed of a large number of episodes which involve conflicts and misunderstandings: and the author provides them. The audience has made a costly transition to a new group, and expects the content to be characteristic of the new community;[13] but it already has ideas as to how stories work, and wants the new expressed in a manner and medium it has already learned to use.

In what follows I want to point to ways in which this suggestion is supported and elaborated in work that I have fairly recently published, other work that I have already in hand, and in projects that still lie ahead.

II

The importance of popular Hellenistic culture for a New Testament writer will perhaps be most readily accepted in the case of Luke's Gospel and Acts, even if it is still debated whether the intended audience was already converted to Christian faith, inquiring, or considered politically useful; or any combination of these. Luke writes for Gentiles, as does Josephus.[14] Luke and Josephus announce very similar aims in similar (and standard) terms,[15] among which is an insistence on the trustworthiness and adequacy of the sources used. However much the author improves on order, and rephrases, and adds imaginative details, he is not expected to create major incidents *de novo* for his audience's pleasure. It is in the speeches placed on his characters' lips that the historian is expected to 'talk with' his hearers, and where his effective fulfilment of their expectations may best be discerned. This is where he shows his awareness of their questions and presuppositions, with such success as his work may be thought or shown to have enjoyed suggesting how well warranted his perceptions may have been.

Josephus' speeches, it turns out, are often variations on a set of religious, political and ethical themes which may be summarized as follows:

God has and exercises foresight (*pronoia*, providence).
He shares this through prophecy and omens, at least sometimes.
He also makes known his will for recurrent situations (in law).
In these ways he is actively kind, eliciting our still 'free' response.

Our response must be virtuous, pious, righteous, worthy . . .
We must bear in mind, reflect on, God's declared or discerned will.
We must maintain ancestral cultus, submit to due authority, preserve 'national' solidarity, but 'human' unity as well.
This obedience may well be costly.

A 'good life' now is our reward.
We may live confidently and hopefully.
We shall be remembered by men, and live with God.

Small failures can be forgiven to the penitent and repentant.
Serious failure is a real possibility, to be carefully avoided.
Punishment and eternal loss could be our lot.[16]

This 'recipe' for his speeches has no clear biblical precedent. Although it has some parallels in Deuteronomic theology (and Josephus does pay particularly careful attention to Deuteronomy itself) there are many contrasts (in Josephus, God and man are allies, *symmachoi*; the Mosaic code is simply a good instance of 'natural law' which informs 'conscience'; omens and dreams are happily accepted; men do not 'love' God; there is the hope of immortality; and so on). Nor do these seem to represent the dominant themes of first-century 'rabbinic' or 'Pharisaic' Judaism (Josephus' own background),[17] though clearly there is some significant overlap. The closest available parallel in fact seems to be provided by the *Roman Antiquities* of Dionysius of Halicarnassus. It is generally accepted that Josephus used this work as his model, and many of his speeches echo those of Dionysius; especially close for instance is that of Aulus Postumius.[18] Dionysius wrote early in the reign of Augustus, but seems to have remained popular. To quote my earlier study:

> Josephus in effect looks at his (Pharisaic) Jewish faith, practice, attitudes, and says to himself, 'These items, properly phrased, should get a fair hearing from people who read and enjoy and approve of Dionysius (and others like him).' The proportion, the emphasis, and quite often the expression are determined, not by their contemporary importance or expression in Palestinian or Hellenistic Judaism, but by the theological, moral and political taste of his (intended) pagan hellenistic readers . . .

And then it must make sense to suggest:

> If Luke . . . says he intends to write the sort of history Josephus says he intends to write . . . there is at least a chance that Luke will also compose speeches in a similar way, perhaps even to a similar recipe. In fact there turns out to be a very close resemblance indeed, and one that covers most of the content of many of the major speeches of Acts.[19]

The speeches of Peter, Gamaliel, Paul *and Stephen* all seem to fall readily under the same set of headings. Luke appears to have a perception of his intended audience's interests, very like that of his contemporary, Josephus.

Not only are Luke's criteria for inclusion very similar, but so are his criteria for *exclusion*. Just as in Josephus, so in the Acts speeches God does not love us, nor we him (nor each other, for that matter). We have no close intimacy with God (in contrast with Romans 8.15, 1 John 1.3, for instance); the only prayer in Acts is very formal, beginning with *despota*, not *abba*, father (and there are parallels to that, again, in Josephus). The only *sōtēria* in Acts is offered in terms of 'forgiveness', with an implicit promise of life to come; on the single occasion when 'justification' is allowed to Paul, it is glossed in terms of forgiveness. No other New Testament term for a new relationship with God through Christ is admitted. But 'repentance' and 'forgiveness' are also the only such terms in Dionysius and Josephus. Then again, there is nothing in the speeches about Christians being a sacrificial or priestly community, and (as often noted) there is little cosmic eschatology (a theme absent from Dionysius, and barely hinted at in Josephus, and then not in speeches).

The positive contents, the individual 'building blocks' of the speeches in Acts are, we are still justified in assuming, tenets which Luke would have expected his fellow Christians to affirm. What I am arguing we may *not* assume is that they offer us any guide as to what even *his* community regarded as important in its own life; still less that his silences tell us what his community did not believe or bother about. (*A fortiori*, he tells us nothing about the earliest Jerusalem community's *kerygma*.) The audience, actual as well as hypothetical, has exercised a controlling influence in the *selection* of what is said.

In further brief support of this major contention I would also draw attention to other speeches in Josephus and in Acts (some of them *not* using the 'recipe'), where it seems to be strongly argued that 'enlightened' pagans, 'good' Gentiles, do display a positive if still not completely adequate relationship with God. Passages such as Acts 17.22–31, and Solomon's Temple Dedication Speech in *Antiquities* are very similar in their affirmation of what many pagans are taken to believe and act on.[20]

If this initial point is granted, then it makes still more sense to see whether the selection of incident and the detailed phraseology used may also reflect the likely expectations of the audience discerned:

> There are characteristics of Luke's work that seem to many readers distinctive when it is compared with Matthew and Mark, and . . . precisely these are prominent in Josephus (and, as it happens, in Dionysius) . . . Luke has a concern for all mankind, especially in the contemporary Roman world; an interest in explaining things for outsiders; an emphasis on prayer and piety; gives added space to female characters; highlights joy, sorrow, and other emotions, especially in the context of repentance; and displays the poor and outcasts in a favourable light (at least, 'the worthy' among them); and . . . has a predilection for travel-narrative, and for (stressing) the strictness of the code (observed).[21]

Luke would again seem to have selected and highlighted under an impetus from his audience as it made its expectations felt, very similar to that to which Josephus was responding.

As already noted, a contemporary Hellenistic audience would not expect a historian to make up incidents *de novo* to entertain or improve it. However rewritten (and the more thoroughly the better) and rearranged,[22] it had to be substantially what was given in his source (just in case anyone checked). A modern historian will almost invariably take his sources to pieces and put them together again, perhaps suggesting a substantially different picture. As T. J. Luce argues, in discussing Livy, precisely this would seem 'irresponsible and wilful' in late antiquity, a procedure which would look like a rejection of his only authoritative material.[23] Nothing in his audience's expectation would have suggested to Luke that he should 'unwrap' Matthew's additions to Mark, and then reuse them. If he had had Matthew as well as Mark in front of him,[24] we would expect a very different outcome from what we in fact find. On the other hand, Luke who uses blocks of Mark and blocks of Q together with perhaps occasional oral memorized material to supplement, and rewrites Mark's passion to produce a tauter and less repetitious narrative, is very much in line with what a moderately sophisticated if not highbrow audience was likely to demand.

Luke's socio-political ethos certainly fits such a setting (and is again similar to that of Josephus). Luke and Josephus both give space to favourable judgements on their religious groups from eminent Romans. Both admit that charges of sedition have been levelled, but both argue that sedition is untrue to the real spirit of their group (so Josephus has to make the Zealots, for instance, effective traitors, not patriots). There may be unrest occasioned by their respective groups, but not initiated by those true to their tenets; disturbances are the totally unjustified reaction of opponents. It is a position most likely to appeal to the wealthier and more established among the early Christian communities, people finding a rewarding purpose in a caring leadership role, an opportunity to exercise a coherent *askēsis* and a real compassion, as well as other talents, within an overarching world view that gave this small-scale activity a feeling of cosmic significance – without risking any damaging change in their actual social position.[25]

III

In some contrast with these would be those more open to a radical Cynic preaching. It is difficult to draw a clear line at this time between 'Stoic-Cynics' (such as Epictetus), and Cynics who, if they philosophize at all, do so in Stoic vein (such as Dio of Prusa, in his post-Sophist period). That Christian evangelists following the instructions in Mark and in Q would have *looked* to others like wandering Cynics has been given fresh attention recently (Hengel, Kee, Theissen).[26] The extent to which they would have *sounded* alike has been given less systematic attention of late, though it was widely noted in New Testament scholarship up to about fifty years ago.[27]

Cynicism was 'more a way of life than a philosophy', at least as open to the ill-educated as to the learned (compare Dio of Prusa, above). It involved a conviction that much was wrong with a consumerist, inegalitarian, authoritarian and hypocritical society, a willingness to protest, and at least in some measure 'opt out'. Our sources suggest it was widespread, touching the countryside as well as the towns, ignoring frontiers; it had something of the sense of mission that Luke suggests for the earliest Christian communities, 'to the uttermost parts of the earth'.[28]

Cynicism included considerable diversity (but then, so too did early Christianity).[29] There are certainly some aspects of early Christianity that even so cannot be found any clear parallels anywhere in the variety of Cynic teaching known to us; this must be conceded at the start. Some Cynics had a sort of 'eschatology', but nothing really resembling that in Q for instance. There was a concern for health, but considerable scepticism (until the next century at least) about miraculous healing. The memory of past teachers was important (as teacher Diogenes of Sinope is a 'liberator'); but there was no ongoing divine power accorded them. There is no Cynic community, no 'Church'. But given these (important) concessions, there are considerable parallels.

Jesus and John scold and rebuke, a distinctive Cynic approach; and Jesus literally 'approaches', goes where people are (unlike non-Cynic philosophers; and, for that matter, unlike other Jewish teachers of whom we know).[30] Audiences are likened to all kind of beasts, and their pretensions to noble ancestry are ridiculed. Symbolic actions are employed, as in many of the *chreiai* ascribed to Diogenes; as do the latter, they disturb contemporary conventions. Positive and distinctive action is expected: Cynic discipleship disrupts ordinary family and civic relationships in a way that the more Stoically minded objected to. Discipleship is hard, and involves a simple life-style, overcoming many attractive temptations. No form of hypocrisy, self-delusion or pretension is tolerated. And the Cynic does not simply 'drop out': he stays around to disturb others, and very likely invite trouble. Cynics were enough of a nuisance to invite the special (hostile) attention of the Flavian emperors. In the first century they seem to have employed at least the rhetoric of theism; their vocation was to serve Zeus as sons serve a father. Their overt aim was not to annoy for the excitement of it, but to show a patience and friendliness that might move the hostile to a more positive response. Care for fellow men mattered much more than any hallowed religious ritual; theirs was a truer piety. This care reflected God's care for them, so they believed; which meant there was no room for anxiety: their few real needs would be met.

The above is, I think, also a fair summary of the drift of much of the Q material; and it is quite clear that first-century listeners would be bound to ask themselves, 'Aren't these (Q preachers) just some new kind of Cynic?', even if they also noted some distinctive features in what they had to say.

It is not the case that this summary is so vague it could include anything. Not all the New Testament writings fall within it. The overall impact of the Lucan writings is other (despite the inclusion of the Q material), and Paul is different again;[31] so too, Hebrews, and Revelation, for instance. But neither does the summary echo all first-century ethical aspirations. Q and Cynicism emerge as having a lot in common.

Perhaps more striking still is the extent to which the special Matthaean material repeats many of these Cynic traits, but also displays further ones. In particular there are the stress on interiority in the Sermon on the Mount, the insistence on living one day at a time, the demand that we choose between two ways, the refusal of oaths, the critique of cultic display, the concern for 'the Good', and the judgement that love for God and neighbour are 'alike'.

There is less to add from Mark: but the criticism of Herod in Chapter 6 invites comparison with the constant Cynic critique of kings and all 'in authority'. (John the Baptist's fatal brush with Herod finds a fascinating parallel in later Cynics' rebukes of Titus for his marital irregularities.) Similarly we have constant controversy, in early chapters as well as in Chapters eleven and twelve; with the talk of true purity in Chapter seven and objections to riches in Chapter ten. With the latter we may compare especially the letter of James; but also add its rebukes to 'double-mindedness' and to all self-indulgence.

It surely cannot be that the early Christians were able to utter all these sentiments without many hearers, many new Christians, noting, 'But that's the sort of thing the Cynics have been saying, ever since I was old enough to stop and listen to them in the market or on the water-front.' It would seem clear that such early Christians at least cannot have been embarrassed by such similarities. (Even Luke admits them into his work in the Q material, while balancing them with more 'politic' material, especially later, in Acts. So even Seneca could quote his Cynic chaplain, Demetrius, while philosophizing Stoically and improving his mind with Epicurus.) But it would seem more likely still that so far from merely not being embarrassed, these early Christians were positively selecting from their traditions of Jesus' teaching that which would 'ring bells' with audiences eager for a religiously based individual radicalism with anti-authoritarian political overtones. The audience has provided many points of contact, and the Christians have happily accepted them.[32]

To repeat, this is not at all to suggest that the Cynics themselves provided the material itself, or any substantial parts of it. Although some parables and other forms are similar, much is distinctively expressed, and looks (to most) clearly Palestinian in origin. But it is to argue again that a very likely audience for the early Christians in the eastern Mediterranean provided important criteria for selection and emphasis; and Christian evangelists, eager to communicate, happily accepted the opportunity to share in conversation rather than restrict themselves to monologue.

It is much harder, because of the state of the data, to tell to what extent Jesus' own original audiences may have been prepared by such Cynic preachers. If we allow some bilingualism, and Cynic determination to go everywhere, and not just to Greek towns, it becomes possible. Certainly Josephus suggests the Cynic 'Fourth Philosophy' had penetrated Palestine well before Jesus' adult years. That is not to say that the coincidences of itinerant style and ethical content may not have been entirely 'fortuitous'. But it is to ask whether they may simply be assumed to have been so.

IV

Although Luke's ideology is conservative, his style strikes most as middlebrow rather than literary (which is not to detract from its effectiveness). Mark's narrative style has even fewer pretensions than has Luke's, and it has seemed to many New Testament historians since the twenties that in Mark we have (as already noted) something *sui generis*, popular narrative (for which we have no surviving parallels) but told to convey a deeply theological message. More recently C. H. Talbert has effectively shown that all the synoptic Gospels, Mark included, have many features in common with surviving cotemporary narrative. I have argued elsewhere that Talbert is wrong, however, in trying to fit the Gospels into some recognizable first-century *genre*; and that the same goes for P. L. Shuler, tracing such theoretical distinctions of *genre* as were discussed at the time.[33] In practice the supposed theoretical distinctions do not hold, as for instance C. B. R. Pelling notes of Plutarch, 'A writer's programmatic statements can be a poor guide to his work . . . (the) biographical genre is an extremely flexible one.'[34]

It is better to remain with the individual common features, 'motifs', the items in the 'narrative vocabulary' used by very different writers in different social settings and literary productions for all kinds of purposes. Quintilian lists about two dozen such motifs,[35] for use in panegyric, while noting how panegyric crosses the provisional distinctions he has suggested. But these motifs recur in history as much as in various kinds of lives, in lectures and poems as well as in discourses. The only feature that seems to be restricted to one recognized *genre* is the long explanatory speech on the lips of a protagonist in a 'history'. For the rest it is possible to discern at least thirty-six recurrent narrative motifs, used in different kinds of storytelling, and also appearing in the synoptic Gospels (and in John). Mark used thirty of them when he pioneered the proclamation of the good news of Jesus in extended narrative form, employing a wide range of the 'narrative vocabulary' to which his audience was accustomed. If Mark, with its Latinisms and adaptation to Roman divorce laws, is taken to be a Roman work, or at least written for a Latin-influenced community, it is particularly intriguing to compare it with the various Romulus sagas available to us. Quintilian seems to imply that some rehearsing of a version of the Romulus story was a legal commonplace; and the apotheosis of any Julian will echo it.[36]

Miracles appear alongside social teaching in the traditions of Romulus, divine voices, significant birds, apparitions. But much of the narrative is concerned with conflict with fellow-countrymen, leaders and family; it is these tensions as such that constitute the dramatic force: their violent resolution is recounted (as in Mark) in only a few lines. Minor characters are flawed in both (Numitor and Faustulus; the disciples, and perhaps the over-awed women); Romulus and Remus themselves are far from perfect. Mark's first audience would be used to such a 'realistic' portrayal, which allows a much readier self-identification on the part of the hearers. Even the 'open secret' of Jesus' identity has a precedent in that of the divine origin of the twins, whose appearance and achievements prompt unresolved questions within the story itself, although 'we' are clearly in the know, not only as to their identity but as to Romulus' significance as Rome's tutelary deity designate. Romulus is supposed to have been killed by a conspiracy of the patricians of his people against him, dying at a time of sudden darkness (in one account, already then acknowledged by soldiers as divine).[37] References to an appearance usually follow in the narratives, but not at once, and (with one surviving exception only)[38] never directly narrated: a third person (Proculus) tells of his experience, and the main narrator remains at one remove. Someone else's message to those concerned is, it seems, the conventional way of narrating an apotheosis.

This is only a brief account of some of the parallels between Mark's narrative vocabulary and that used in one Roman saga; similar parallels, and others besides, can be found in other stories, Greek as well as Roman. On this basis we gain a much clearer idea of how Mark and his audience were likely to have understood each other. Mark 16.8 would be an entirely comprehensible ending; the rebukes to the original disciples would not have been seen as a polemic against them or their successors; and the open secret surrounding Jesus would probably not be seen as a rather weak response to awkward questions about his initial failure to persuade more people, still less as a counter-balance to the whole mass of miracle-stories that Mark includes.

Many recent analyses of Mark (and of Matthew and Luke) have supposed that each evangelist's 'real' message is conveyed very obliquely and allusively. It is by no means impossible that contemporary redactors did use such devices to *supplement* the main case they were making: but they would also state it clearly and forcefully, by selection and by editorial statement. All recent analyses of Mark as author presuppose that he could expect his audience to discern the drift of his narrative. If that is right at all, then it is as just outlined above that they would most likely have taken it. Had Mark wanted them to take some other reading, he would soon have learned that he needed to write it differently.[39]

It is perhaps worth adding that there is no indication in the literature available to us of any *genre* of 'pure aretalogy', just as there is no negative evidence for such an aretalogical account of Jesus being here countered by Mark in some curiously ineffective way. (That Mark is, on the other hand, stressing the cost of discipleship, for all the availability of miraculous power, *is* entirely clear. This he says clearly and unambiguously;[40] as well as supporting the message by his selection of narrative *pericopai* and very likely by his shaping of them.)

V

It is perhaps in Pauline studies that scholars have been most willing to consider the question of the audience the writer indicates. The Corinthian correspondence in particular clearly implies a two-way communication, even though we have only one side of it, and cannot even tell for sure whether the issues Paul refers to (e.g. 'It is good for a man not to touch a woman') simply pick up points the Corinthian community has itself raised; or are quotations from his own earlier teaching perhaps misunderstood; or constitute the gist of his present response. Although we know there was an audience responding, we are still left to reconstruct imaginatively the kind of response that was forthcoming, the sort of 'feedback' Paul was really receiving. Our difficulty is illustrated by the variety of interpretations the commentators suggest.[41] Given a few allusive words like *sophia, mystērion, teleios, gnōsis* in 1 Corinthians 2 and 6, and some unspecified problems over resurrection in Chapter Fifteen, it is possible to spin from those points many different but coherent and very impressive structures that embrace the remainder of the Corinthian correspondence, and maybe all the rest of Paul's writings left to us. It is as easy as it is to make an overheard telephone conversation mean almost anything by filling in the silences to suit one's own expectations.

Without claiming to have read all the discussions of 'gnosticism at Corinth', in none of what has come my way am I aware of any systematic attempt to discover whether there is any *external* evidence for any such pre-Christian or early Christian tendency there, or even any likelihood of it. My own reading in Hellenistic literature of the second half of the first century has afforded no support for any such picture.

J. M. Robinson writes, 'This same withdrawal to inwardness or despair of the world from which the gnostic stance emerged swept not only through early Christianity to produce Christian Gnosticism, but also through late antiquity in general, thus producing forms of Gnosticism outside Christianity.'[42] For the withdrawal to inwardness, and even for the despair I think there is *some* evidence.[43] For any 'Gnosticism' so named, the earliest firm pagan reference is in Plotinus in the third century.[44] Just possibly Celsus in the second century may have had gnostic heretics in mind, though Origen is not sure; but Celsus saw them as evidence of internal Christian divisions, not of assimilation to non-Christian trends.[45] Apart from these two, arguments for any widespread Gnosticism in the first century (Christian or non-Christian or both) demand a willingness to read back from late second-century Christians (Irenaeus, Hippolytus) and from the likely earlier second-century originals of the third-century Nag Hammadi documents, to otherwise quite unevidenced mid-first-century movements and institutions.

We have in fact many discussions of religion and of 'superstition' from the late first and early second centuries. In none of them so far, to my knowledge, has even the keenest proponent of a pervasive first-century Gnosticism found any evidence for it whatsoever. Inwardness (and possibly despair) there may be; but Gnosticism in any recognizable form is nowhere to be found. This is not at all what we would expect, were these at all widespread gnostic cults. Such despair of the social and physical world, such refusal to exercise even an inner 'existential' freedom would have constituted a prime example of the 'superstition' that so many of our writers condemn. Yet no such reference is anywhere to be found. Astrology is discussed, and belief in moody deities easily offended and hard to placate, the causes of sickness and other ills: but the concerns involved are entirely of this world, as is the 'salvation' sought.[46] When cults are mentioned they are the civic ones of Rome and Greece and other areas, the 'mystery' developments of them; or the sophisticated religion of philosophers. This is so for Philo, Josephus, Pliny elder (and junior), Seneca, Epictetus, Juvenal, the historians, Plutarch, Lucian. Dio of Prusa has much to criticize in his various *Discourses* addressed to cities of the east Mediterranean (including Tarsus), and theological issues are frequently raised. His own beliefs are, in their logic, fundamentally opposed to the logic of Gnosticism as usually characterized. Deity for Dio is creative and benevolent and providential; physical and 'spiritual' welfare are closely linked; we should accept responsibility for one another; the only 'spiritual powers' that threaten our integrity are pride, greed, pleasure, all of which may be controlled by divine reason.[47] Yet there is no hint that he is combating any very different proposed *definition* of the human situation, as really demanding some saving knowledge to enable release. He is insisting that the problems as commonly perceived can be dealt with. In particular, *Discourses* eight, nine and ten imagine Diogenes at or near Corinth, excoriating all and sundry for their folly, wickedness and intemperance. There is no suggestion here of antiquarian research, it is clearly Dio's own rebuke to his contemporaries. He claims to be dealing with all their failings; yet, again, not once is any 'gnostic' delusion even touched in passing.

As already allowed, this is not to claim an entire absence of tendencies to inward withdrawal and despair in the literature of the age. In his thirtieth *Discourse, Charidemus*, Dio outlines three possible views of the world. The first is deeply pessimistic, humans are the punished descendants of the Titans, and the world a penal colony. But this 'myth' seems clearly Orphic and Pythagorean, death is the one but effective release (with no problems to follow, not even 're-imprisonment' in this instance), and (again) philosophic reason is the only effective present solace. Dio does not seem to suggest that even this view was all that widespread; rather his second view, of a gradual fall of mankind from its original kinship with the gods, in a world that invited self-indulgence and undue attachment, would seem to represent the majority. The third is similar to that of Epictetus, his teacher: we are at a banquet and spectacle with a friendly host, whose company we should enjoy abstemiously. The 'Zoroastrian' Stoic cosmogonic myth of *Discourse* thirty-six could of course be read 'gnostically', as could any imaginative construction: but it expresses a faith in a good and beautiful and guided universe.

The social and psychological *tendencies* that underlie second-century Gnosticism are surely already operative. There is no sign at all that the second-century *symptoms* have yet appeared in such a way as to create a demand or even a possibility of comprehension of such mythology in Paul's audiences. The tendencies are sometimes detected for instance in Philo of Alexandria, in his often 'escapist' spirituality (though he did maintain his social and political concern),[48] and in his ideas of intermediate 'powers' between the ineffable God and his world. Yet even Philo's most 'other-worldly' – seeming theology is basically un-gnostic in its tendency. When we consider the human situation 'from our end', contact with the ineffable God seems impossible. Considered, however theoretically, from 'God's side', it is quite different. There is no symmetry. God remains providentially all powerful, the creator, sustainer and ruler of Jewish belief, dealing with us. The distance only appears when *we* try to deal with him, or even consider dealing with him, and then he is 'incomprehensible'. The upshot remains rootedly 'un-gnostic'.[49]

The same emerges in Plutarch's pagan platonizing, for instance in his *de iside et osiride*. As spiritualizing allegorical interpretation of the cult, the tendency is again towards an escape inwards. We pray for knowledge of the gods (*epistēmē*), as far as that is possible, yet not that alone, but that as the best of many other good things, in a world about which God (*sic*) knows and cares, a world in which God can be effectively if still very partially mirrored.[50]

This last reference allows me to repeat a point that I value; though it is not original to me, I would suggest it is more significant than others who have noted it seem to allow. In 1 Corinthians 13 Paul talks about the inadequacy of our present knowledge of God; for now we see puzzling reflections in a mirror, 'then' our knowledge will be complete. Plutarch uses precisely this terminology to make a very similar point, in his *de iside et osiride*.[51] Where we do find Paul expecting his audience to think about what is involved in *gnōsis*, 'knowledge of God', it is in terms of this sophisticated philosophy of religion, quite distinct in its pious 'agnosticism' from any later gnostic claims to privileged insight. Paul does not argue or explain the point, he simply seems to suppose his audience will accept it. (If this chapter thirteen is an inserted set-piece, the point is even stronger, for he would have had ample opportunity to learn that he was himself being 'enigmatic'.)[52]

VI

Supposing then that our independent evidences for audiences for the first Christians' attempts to communicate do afford us at least some 'controls', of the kind I have been suggesting, the further question arises as to whether that enables us even so to attain to any 'real' and effective understanding of the New Testament documents. May it not be the case that the more firmly we set those writings in the thought-world of the first century, the more unintelligible (in any 'deep' sense) they become for us? This has of course been strongly urged of late by a number of concerned scholars.[53]

This is not the place to discuss the philosophical basis for cultural relativism.[54] Two concrete illustrations of the kind of characterization of divergencies between the first and the twentieth centuries may suffice: In those days 'when things go wrong . . . the obvious response will be, not to investigate the working of impersonal secondary causes, which will not be recognized to exist, but to discover what evil supernatural power is at work' and, 'In the Western world, both popular culture and the culture of the intelligentsia has come to be dominated by the human and natural sciences to such an extent that supernatural causation or intervention in the affairs of this world has become, for the majority of people, simply incredible'.[55] Yet with that contrast between the two worlds we may compare for instance this note from Philo:

> The view . . . is widely current that all things in the world run along automatically (*automatōs*), independently of anyone to guide them, and that the human mind by itself established arts, professions, laws, customs and rules of right treatment both of men and animals on the part of the state and in our conduct whether as individuals or as members of communities.[56]

(The word *automatōs* would seem from Josephus' use of it in this kind of context to be fairly commonplace.) This does not suggest that there is no difference between our century and the first: clearly we have a fuller understanding of the regularities that obtain 'automatically', and are able to use them with great technical (if not social or moral) proficiency. What this, and the many other available illustrations do show is that it is always a question of *more or less* similarity or difference.

This then brings me to my final substantial suggestion. Among the least useful starting points for understanding someone else are a literal translation of a religious myth, rubrics for a cultic act, the names for bits of military hardware, and the career structure of his civil service. But it is these kinds of things that tend to figure in accounts of the first century. Instead, what we need if we are to hope to understand, is some idea of the attitudes of the people involved: not what they chanted in their temple, but what they (perhaps variously) thought they were doing, and what they felt about it all. It is not the legal niceties of *confarreatio* that tell us what marriage was like, but discovering whether wives and husbands talked to each other, cared for the children, cared about each other. Epictetus on enjoying the company of toddlers, on proper care for a sick daughter, on a father's involvement in coping with a new-born baby, and later in getting it off to school, tells us more about what he *may* have meant by calling Zeus father,[57] than will a note about a patrician father technically still owning his children, with power of life and death. Paul's anguished little note about his women colleagues, Euodia and Syntyche, tells us more about the relations of women and men in the early churches than does his strained attempt to regulate headgear (or hairstyles). Recent attempts at social analysis (Judge, Grant, Theissen, Meeks, Kee) are a considerable step forward. But even more important as an initial stage, it seems to me, is a fuller social description which goes beyond religious systems and political and social structures and the chronicling of kings and generals, and at least tries to show something of what it was like to *live* this way, relating to other people.[58]

VII

The title for this essay, 'Ears to hear', could, on some interpretations, have been very ill-chosen. The ensuing sequence in Mark 4, alluding to Isaiah 6, 'hearing they may hear and not understand', could suggest that Mark (and other early Christians using that theme from Isaiah: Matthew, Luke, John, Paul) cared nothing for communication. Perhaps they saw their task simply as a matter of having their say, and others could take it or leave it. It would, however, seem much more likely to be evidence for the frustration of determined efforts to 'connect', a puzzlement as to why at the end of strenuous attempts to discover how to talk with people, some were persuaded and some were not. Every effort had to be made, nonetheless, to ensure that they could not merely 'listen', but hear. Only then could you suppose you had done God's will, and the rest was up to him. If the evidence briefly displayed here suggests any concern on the part of early Christians to communicate, then the 'take it or leave it' interpretation for Mark 4 and similar passages will not hold; and in that case such passages can only indicate the alternative intention, a painstaking attention to what their contemporaries were able to 'hear', an attention we need to emulate if we are to hope ourselves to understand the first Christians' attempts to communicate and if we are to hope to share and enrich our understanding with others.

NOTES

1 Perhaps there is a reaction against 'classical' form criticism's stress on the community, as exemplified by such scholars as K. L. Schmidt, R. Bultmann, M. Dibelius. Even those who have tried to take in more of the contemporary cultural scene (and not concentrated on the Christian and Jewish traditions behind the Gospels) seem to see the authors as responding in solitude to this albeit wide range of stimuli;

see for instance, J. Rohde, *Rediscovering the Teaching of the Evangelists*, London 1968; N. Perrin, *What is Redaction Criticism?* London 1970; W. H. Kelber, *The Passion in Mark* (Philadelphia 1976); C. H. Talbert, *What is a Gospel?* Philadelphia 1977; P. L. Shuler, *A Genre for the Gospels*, Philadelphia 1982. We are looking for 'the hand of the author' (ibid., p. 33).

2 N. R. Petersen, *Literary Criticism for New Testament Critics*, Philadelphia, 1978, and in other writing, uses the a-historical procedures to make fruitful suggestions about Mark, for instance; but does not ask questions about the contemporary audience. F. Kermode, *The Genesis of Secrecy*, Cambridge, Mass., and London 1979, allows for the distinction, pp. 162ff, n. 20, only to pass it by; so, too, H.-J. Klauck, 'Die erzählerische Rolle der Jünger im Markus Evangelium', *Nov.T.* xxiv, 1 (1982), pp. 22–5.

3 T. Rajak, *Josephus* (London 1983), pp. 62f; Pliny Junior, *Letters* VII. 17; Cicero, *Atticus* 2.1.1–2; E. Best, *Mark, The Gospel as Story*, Edinburgh, 1983, acknowledges that the Gospel of Mark is most likely to have been composed in constant interaction between author and congregation, pp. 13, 19, etc., though he does not consider the likely wider expectations of the audience.

4 Josephus, *Life*, 361–7.

5 Quintilian, *Institutes*, dedication and preface.

6 Dio, *Discourses* 11.6; 57.10–12; 42.4–5.

7 Dio, *Discourses* 32.9; cf. 42.4–5, referred to above.

8 For example, Philo, *de congressu* 64–7, *de abrahamo* 20.

9 Quintilian, *Institutes* III, viii; but the whole of III is relevant.

10 Compare H. Koester, *Introduction to the New Testament*, I: *History, Culture and Religion of the Hellenistic Age*, Philadelphia and Berlin 1982, on the 'public' and 'international' 'character of cultural and intellectual life'. Dio says, 'almost all men are acquainted with my speeches, and they distribute them broadcast in all directions . . . almost all report my speeches to one another . . . (*Disc.* 42.5). He talks himself of roaming everywhere, among Greeks and barbarians, in towns and in the countryside (*Disc.* 1.50f; 13.10ff, 29). Both Quintilian and Pliny jun. expect to have to address very ordinary people in legal pleading. Whatever scholarly consensus may obtain to the contrary, I feel that the *onus probandi* lies with those who would deny any widespread contact between 'aristocratic culture' whose remains are known to us, and ordinary people. E. Best, op. cit., cites G. Kennedy, 'Some knowledge of rhetorical techniques and conventions would have filtered down to the lower levels of society and would have coloured the expectations, perhaps unconsciously, of those who listened to early Christian preachers . . . ' (p. 101f), from G. Kennedy in W. O. Walker, *The Relationships among the Gospels* (San Antonio, Texas 1978), p. 184. It is also worth noting that studies of the social mix among early Christians by E. A. Judge, R. M. Grant, G. Theissen, W. Meeks would all include an important wealthier and more educated component.

11 R. Brown, *The Community of the Beloved Disciple*, London 1979; C. H. Dodd, *The Interpretation of the Fourth Gospel*, Cambridge 1953.

12 J. Habermas, *Communication and the Evolution of Society*, London, 1979; and 'A Reply to my Critics', in J. B. Thompson and D. Held (eds.) *Habermas: Critical Debates*, London 1982; but also, for example, M. Argyle, *The Psychology of Interpersonal Behaviour*, London 1967; J. B. Biggs, *Information and Human Learning*, Melbourne 1968. L. Wittgenstein, *Philosophical Investigations*, Oxford 1958; J. L. Austin, *How to do Things with Words*, Oxford 1962; J. R. Searle, *Speech Acts*, Cambridge 1969, and other writing.

13 E. Best, again, op. cit., chs. 5 and 20. I have myself compiled a collection (as yet unpublished) of first-century texts under the title *Strangely Familiar*, which in fact also show many other areas of *at least apparent* overlap between early Christian thought and its expression, and that of the surviving Greco-Roman literature.

14 Compare F. G. Downing, 'Ethical Pagan Theism and the Speeches in Acts', *NTS* 27 (1981), pp. 544–63; and 'Common Ground with Paganism in Luke and in Josephus', *NTS*, 28 (1982), pp. 546–59; and, for example, J. M. Hull, *Hellenistic Magic and the Synoptic Tradition* (London 1974), ch. 6, 'Luke'.

15 See F. G. Downing, 'Redaction Criticism: Josephus' *Antiquities* and the Synoptic Gospels (II)', *JSNT* 9, 1980.

16 F. G. Downing, 'Ethical Pagan Theism . . . ' art. cit., pp. 549f.

17 At least as discerned by E. P. Sanders, *Paul and Palestinian Judaism*, London 1977; F. G. Downing, 'Ethical Pagan Theism', art. cit., p. 551.

18 Dionysius, *R.A.* VI, 6. 1—9.5.

19 F. G. Downing, art. cit., p. 553f.

20 Josephus, *Antiquities* VIII 102–29; see F. G. Downing, 'Common Ground with Paganism . . . ', art. cit.

21 F. G. Downing, 'Redaction Criticism . . . II', art. cit., p. 32.

22 Compare A. Pelletier, *Flavius Josèphe, Adapteur de la lettre d'Aristée*, Paris 1962.

23 T. J. Luce, *Livy* (Princeton 1977), pp. 143ff.

24 As suggested, for example, by M. D. Goulder, *Midrash and Lection in Matthew*, London 1974; J. Drury, *Tradition and Design in Luke's Gospel*, London 1976.

25 Compare D. L. Mealand, *Poverty and Expectation in the Gospels* (London 1980), ch. 2. Note also the discussion in the following: D. L. Mealand, 'Philo of Alexandria's Attitude to Riches', *ZNW* 69 (1978); T. E. Schmidt, 'Hostility to Wealth in Philo of Alexandria', *JSNT* 19 (1983); and forthcoming rejoinders in *JSNT* by D. L. Mealand and F. G. Downing. It is quite clear that *in context* the Lucan warnings against riches and idealization of poverty operate in the same kind of way as such sentiments in Seneca, and Dionysius of Halicarnassus. They are not evacuated of meaning, but they are styled for the rich. (*Per contra*, R. J. Cassidy, *Jesus, Politics and Society*, New York 1978,

and R. J. Cassidy, ed., *Political Issues in Luke–Acts*, New York 1983.)

26 M. Hengel, *The Charismatic Leader and his Followers* (Edinburgh 1981), pp. 25–7; H. C. Kee, *Christian Origins in Sociological Perspective* (London 1980), pp. 68–70; G. Theissen, 'Wanderradikalismus . . . ' ZThK 70 (1973), and *The First Followers of Jesus* (London 1978), pp. 16f.

27 E. Hatch, *The Influence of Greek Ideas on Christianity*, London 1890; S. Dill, *Roman Society from Bero to Marcus Aurelius*, London 1905; W. R. Halliday, *The Pagan Background of Early Christianity*, London 1925; D. B. Dudley, *A History of Cynicism*, London 1937.

28 '*heōs an epi to hustaton apelthēs tēs gēs*' (Dio, *Disc.* 13.9; cf. Acts 1.8).

29 Compare J. D. G. Dunn, *Unity and Diversity in the New Testament*, London 1977. For what follows, see my 'Cynics and Christians', *NTS* 30 (1984); A. J. Malherbe, *The Cynic Epistles* (Missoula, Montana 1977), 'Introduction', pp. 1–2.

30 Compare especially V. K. Robbins, 'Mark 1.14–20: an interpretation at the intersection of Jewish and Graeco-Roman traditions', *NTS* 28 (1982), pp. 220–36; and (id.) 'Summons and Outline in Mark., *Nov. T.* xxiii, 2, 1981.

31 Cf., for example, H. D. Betz, *Galatians*, Philadelphia 1979; H. Conzelmann, *I Corinthians*, Philadelphia 1975; W. A. Meeks, *The First Urban Christians*, New Haven and London 1983; S. K. Stowers, *The Diatribe and Paul's Letter to the Romans*, Chico 1981.

32 F. G. Downing, 'The Politics of Jesus', *Modern Churchman* 25, 1982.

33 C. H. Talbert and P. L. Shuler, opera citeriora; F. G. Downing, 'Contemporary Analogies to the Gospels and Acts: "Genre" or "Motifs"?', in C. Tuckett (ed.), *Synoptic Studies*, Sheffield 1984.

34 C. B. R. Pelling, 'Plutarch's Adaptation of his Source Material', *JHS* 1980; compare his previous 'Plutarch's Method of Work in the Roman Lives', *JHS* 1979.

35 Quintilian, *Institutes* III, viii but note all of III, iv–viii).

36 Quintilian, *Institutes* IV, vii. 5; Seneca, *Apocolocyntosis*, 1.

37 Livy, *History*, I, 15–16.

38 Ovid, *Metamorphoses* xiv, 806–27 is the only exception I could find. In *Fasti* ii, 491–512 he follows the otherwise normal line. I hope to publish somewhere a fuller account under the title 'Hearing Mark read in Rome.'

39 In fact, as already noted, E. Best, *Mark*, op. cit., understands it much as contemporary narrative suggests it would have been taken, in my judgement.

40 See the discussion in Best, *Mark*, op.cit., and also his *Following Jesus*, Sheffield 1981. In discussions I have had with various kindly critics the question has often re-emerged, as to why, if Mark is responding to the narrative expectations of, say, Roman hearers, he includes so much material with a Jewish legal or eschatological flavour. I have already suggested (claiming Best's support) that the material is likely to have been provided from within Mark's own community; and I have also noted the contemporary importance of faithfulness to

sources. I would not expect Mark to include every last scrap of available matter; but I suggest he and his community would expect every important kind of material to be represented. The argument is – as are most in this field – somewhat circular; but, as Best for example points out (against H. C. Kee's thesis in *The Community of the New Age*), Mark can be seen apparently 'toning down' some of the eschatological material (Best, *Mark*, op. cit., p. 42), which would indicate on any thesis some pressure other than 'author-pleasingness'. My case by no means demands that Mark's only motive be to write a good Roman story; only that, within the constraints of the community tradition, this is what he seems to have done.

41 See n. 31 above.

42 J. M. Robinson (ed.), *The Nag Hammadi Library* (Leiden 1977), p. 6.

43 See, for example, Plutarch, *de iside et osiride*, and *de superstitione*; and see below.

44 Id., op. cit., p. 8. Compare E. Yamauchi, *Pre-Christian Gnosticism*, London 1973; D. Winslow, 'Religion and the early Roman Empire', in S. Benko and J. J. O'Rourke, eds., *Early Church History*, London 1971.

45 Origen, *contra celsum* III, xiii; V, lxi; VI, xxiv.

46 See especially, Plutarch, *de superstitione, Moralia* 164E–171F; but see also Juvenal, *Satires*; Pliny sen., *Natural History*; Epictetus, *Dissertations*; Dio's account of religious options, *Disc.* 30, *Charidemus* (see further, below); and Cicero's *de natura deorum* for the previous century; but also Philo and Josephus; and for the second century, Lucian.

47 Dio, *Disc.* 4.82–139; *Disc.* 25.

48 See references in n. 25 above.

49 On this asymmetry, as just one striking example, *de legatione* 118, *thatton gar an eis anthrōpon theon ē eis theon anthrōpon metabalein.* Philo's 'ungnostic' stance appears especially clearly in *de gigantibus*, where it might most readily have appeared, and in *de praemiis et poenis*, with its very this-worldly eschatology.

50 *de iside et osiride, Moralia* 351CD, 381–3.

51 I Corinthians 13.12; Plutarch, *Moralia* 381–3, as above.

52 See F. G. Downing, 'Reflecting the First Century', *Expository Times* 95, 6 (1984).

53 For example, D. E. Nineham, *The Use and Abuse of the Bible*, London 1976; and various writers in J. Hick (ed.) *The Myth of God Incarnate*, London 1977.

54 See F. G. Downing, 'Our Access to other Cultures, Past and Present', *Modern Churchman*, winter 1977; 'Games, Families, the Public, and Religion', *Philosophy*, January 1972; 'Meanings', in M. Hooker and C. Hickling (eds), *What about the New Testament?* London 1975; J. Barton, 'Cultural Relativism' I and II, *Theology* lxxxii, pp. 686 and 687.

55 D. E. Nineham, *Use*, op. cit., p. 22; F. Young, in J. Hick, *Myth*, op. cit., p. 31.

56 Philo, *de leg. all.* III.30, Loeb; for other references, F. G. Downing, 'Our Access . . .', art.cit., p. 31.

57 Epictetus, *Diss.* III, xx. 70–4, etc.

58 This is the intention of my collection of texts, *Strangely Familiar*, referred to in note 13 above, and explains my hope that it may in due course be published.

7

Trying to be a New Testament Theologian

LESLIE HOULDEN

My question is: what can the study of New Testament theology contribute to the study and formulation of Christian doctrine, that is, to the theological task in the wider sense? There is no denying that the subject is at present problematic. It was formerly the crown of the New Testament scholar's career to write a theology of the New Testament, comprehending in a unified vision the ideas hitherto put forward in relation to discrete topics but now seen as contributions to a whole. Even when death or exhaustion has not supervened, there has been a decline in the number of those trusting their wisdom enough to undertake such a project, and some would not now see it as part of their craft.

It is not simply a question of trusting one's wisdom. The subject itself has long been more than a little ambiguous. Is New Testament theology[1] simply one aspect of the rigorously historical study of these writings, limiting itself to a descriptive role? Or is it a kind of theology, setting out to give an account of Christian doctine as revealed and normative, but in terms related to and based upon the New Testament? Even when it sets out on the former path, it has a way in practice of straying on to the latter;[2] but at the level of theory the ambiguity remains. The most severely historical kind of New Testament theology in fact has a doctrinal role, if only in stimulating the imagination theologically. So it may be that New Testament theology is always something of a hybrid, even if only by implication.

From the time when New Testament studies set up as an independent enterprise, and were released from merely backing up doctrine, New Testament theology has been not only of the descriptive but also of the theologically more positive kind, an account of the Christian faith from a New Testament perspective. So whatever the proportions of New Testament studies and doctrine may be, and whatever the precise nature of each in a particular case, New Testament theology is New Testament scholarship looking in some way in a doctrinal direction. It compels the specialists to turn their eyes towards a neighbouring field. If they do so now, they may be forgiven for shrinking back into the relative order and safety of their own familiar territory. The land of doctrine is not a tidy or a pleasant sight. Who knows on what principles matters are conducted there? Are its inhabitants committed to expounding the authoritative doctrines of Christianity, a body of belief achieved at Nicaea and Chalcedon or Trent or Vatican II? Are they interested in the New Testament evidence in a manner dictated by the items of the dogmatic theologian's traditional agenda?[3] If so, then the New Testament scholars feel a professional unease: they feel that the achievements of the dogmatic process in Christian history were in various ways parasitic on the New Testament, and they are conscious that their present ways of handling it threaten the methods whereby those doctrinal beliefs were reached. There is a risk of gaff-blowing, even of calling in question the whole business of forming theology on the basis of the New Testament.[4] It is not a thing for a courteous visitor to do.

Or are those who live in the land of doctrine committed to something much closer to philosophy of religion? In that case, New Testament scholars find it hard to discover a point of attachment, yet they know that such a point must be found. Neither their professional equipment nor the documents which are the subject of their study give them much skill when it comes to such fundamental doctrinal reasoning. It is outside their reach; for however great their academic detachment, in so far as they are practitioners of the Christian tradition, they work from the inside.

In fact, all the doctrine-dwellers (so it seems to outsiders) act according to their own lights. Compared to New Testament scholars, they seem an anarchic lot. Even within a single church tradition, the subject appears to lack clear criteria, even clear subject-matter. Where it is (essentially even if disguised) commentary on decisions and formulations arrived at elsewhere, then it is plainly a dependent enterprise; and, unless there is to be an assumption of divine guidance transcending human activity, its purity is marred by knowledge of the political and cultural factors affecting the process by which the formulations came to birth. Dogmas do not drop from heaven any more than scriptures. Where it is more abstract or independent in its stance,[5] then it is liable to be more or less cut off from that church setting which, whatever its inconveniences, seems to be doctrine's proper location.

Sometimes, doctrine seeks to be a looser, more varied pursuit than I have so far recognized. It may reckon to draw on resources of many kinds, in effect from the general intellectual climate. There will be a broad dependence on the prevailing philosophical atmosphere, a recognition of 'what cannot now be said by reasonable people'. There will be an awareness of the appropriate church tradition, and probably of the Christian tradition as a whole. There will be sensitivity to hermeneutical procedures, enabling the past and the present to be stirred into the mixing-bowl from which acceptable doctrine may emerge.[6]

Doctrine scholars of this persuasion are hopeful and co-operative by disposition, and of all styles of doctrinal study this one is the most likely to turn, in a spirit which both gives and seeks sympathy, to New Testament scholarship. Starting from the other side, such doctrine scholars as these are the nearest counterpart to the New Testament theologians, those most likely to listen to their voice and not seek simply to bend them to their predetermined needs. It is true that they have other bridges, too, to build and maintain, but they cannot avoid the search for some satisfactory way of regarding and then using the New Testament, both as a collection of writings from the start of the Christian tradition and as a powerful presence throughout that tradition's course. There is no avoiding the conclusion, however, that if doctrinal scholars seek such help, they are likely, in present circumstances, to go away either empty-handed or with a gift of raw, undeveloped material unaccompanied by instructions for its use. If the land of doctrine looks to would-be New Testament theologians bewildering in its uncertainty and diversity, New Testament scholars easily seem naive and unreflective when they aspire to theological activity. They keep running for cover in enclosed historical or linguistic investigations. They will not come out with clear guidance on what is to be done with their deliverances. And when they speak theologically, not only are they too wedded to New Testament words and ideas, but they seem unwilling to reckon with so many considerations which are plainly important theologically.[7] Sometimes they just disclaim responsibility, in a way which the doctrine scholars find feeble and infuriating, for it impedes their own work.

There are of course reasons more domestic to New Testament scholarship itself for the reticence which attends the pursuit of New Testament theology. Everything pushes in the direction of work and perception which are analytic and historically limited – analytic and particularized as more attention is legitimately given to the theological outlook of individual New Testament writers and less to ideas and terms across the New Testament as a whole. If the New Testament is treated thus, what can a New Testament theologian contribute but an account of each of the writers in turn? Historically limited, as the life and thought of the New Testament period are perceived with increasing vividness and fullness and with the aid of ever sharper tools such as those derived from sociology and anthropology. All these trends reduce interest in and facility for handling the New Testament as the fount of a tradition and as itself a witness to theological truth.

However, in some aspects of redaction criticism and other associated techniques of gospel study, there is intensified pressure in a clearly theological direction. What is not so evident, at least at first sight, is how this brand of theological interest, rigorously historical as it is, can contribute to New Testament theology in any comprehensive sense, especially if such theology is itself to contribute to theology understood more widely. Still, there is undoubtedly here a lever upon which we may seek to lean in order to shift the dead weight that now inhibits New Testament theology from movement. In due course, I shall make use of it.

The overwhelmingly historical orientation of New Testament studies is not only a deterrent to the pursuit of New Testament theology in principle. It is also the source of dissatisfaction with such attempts as have been made in the past. Those who have done New Testament theology by the apparently direct method of distinguishing and relating themes found in the writings themselves, usually attributing a key role to some among them, have fallen victim to increased sensitivity to the culture-bound nature of those themes, as they are expressed in first-century words and ideas.[8] To work with those ideas and words in propounding theological patterns for today is to impose upon them senses and connections which they never had in the New Testament itself and to make assumptions about the canon which need bold argument if they are to avoid the charges of anachronism and arbitrariness.

The brave attempt to distil from the New Testament a theology for our times which goes by the name of demythologization runs into comparable difficulties. For the New Testament writers, what *we* may call the essence of their teaching and the myth in which, to our eyes, it was clothed formed a unity. There must then be now a sense of impropriety in severing the one from the other and claiming the palatable aspects of the New Testament writers' work (and usually in fact that of only a selection of them) as a fair account of New Testament theology. In that way, while it avoids the mere retailing of New Testament words and ideas, a programme of demythologization falls equally under the charges of anachronism and arbitrariness.[9] From another angle, it is yet one more in the long line[10] of accounts of New Testament teaching which ruthlessly impose upon it a later viewpoint, perhaps highly commendable in itself but found appealing on other grounds besides its supposed presence in the New Testament.

If recent experience is anything to go by, there seems to be no way of escaping from the extreme difficulty of making legitimate use of the New Testament theologically if we are at the same time to be faithful to historical method. Where attempts have been made to present the theology of the New Testament, it now often seems that there was a blurred historical focus, some degree of failure to reckon with the writings in their own right and in their own setting. This is not simply an intellectual failure, something to earn a historian's rebuke. It is also a moral failure; for it involves a refusal to hear what the ancient writer wished to say, an insistence that he speak to our condition and dance to our tune. Even if we stick close to his words, they are almost inevitably bent to needs and purposes other than those of their original setting, often by the mere fact of their removal from the total social and cultural context in which they were written.

It is possible to cut the knot by the simple expedient of dropping faithfulness to historical method when it comes to making theological use of the New Testament documents, and so confining historical work on them to its own strict and narrow concerns. It may be done not, as so often, by sheer inadvertence or out of some atavistic dogmatism, but in a spirit of high sophistication.[11] We may hold that the New Testament is a text, words on paper, which we should receive and attend to simply as they strike us. Interpretation is then not an academic but an aesthetic experience, though no doubt with subsequent moral or intellectual effect. If I read the story of the walk to Emmaus, I am not to immerse myself in questions about its possible source and literary affinities, its vocabulary and place in Lucan thought or among the resurrection stories. Such concerns will divert me from it simply as a text, push me into matters which lie behind it rather than within it. Rather, I must let the text as text work its will with me, seize me if it can, and move me by the sheer power of its structure and wording: thus will its message be heard. We note that there is here no strictly theological interest. It is not a matter of reversion to the uncritical use of texts in support of doctrines. If there is theological fruit from this approach, then it is inchoate, indirect, and by way of the stimulation of the theological imagination.

New Testament scholars will not easily content themselves with such a solution – for both the worst and the best of reasons. The worst of reasons is fear of the elimination of New Testament scholarship from the business of theological interpretation. If New Testament scholarship were to be mainly confined to purely historical exegesis in its various aspects – and this is perilously near to being the case – then there would be a serious price to pay at the practical level: in terms of even greater isolation from other theological disciplines, the loss of any claim to what may, in a Benthamite spirit, be called usefulness, and ultimately an intelligible threat from the paymasters of the academic world: for why should this little collection of first-century texts, if that is the perspective in which they are deliberately and exclusively being viewed, merit more than a pittance from any public or private coffers, more than a fraction of the academic resources still devoted to them?

Fear is a low reason for discontent with the removal from theological reflection on the New Testament of historical study in its many aspects. A higher reason is a conviction that the understanding of the historical realities involved in the composing of a text is an enrichment to general appreciation and neither an impediment nor a diversion. Not only is it a brake upon sheer error but there is, not necessarily but potentially, a continuum between historical knowledge and even the quasi-aesthetic and very personal 'grasping' of the text which I described. Such knowledge constitutes a salutary discipline which purifies and enhances rather than impedes appreciation.

If then we exclude the dropping of historical method as a

satisfactory way out of our difficulties, it remains inadequate to withdraw, in deference to that method, from serious theological concern. There is indeed one peculiarly problematic reason for discomfort in settling for the self-sufficiency and self-containedness of the historical study of the New Testament. It is the question of the relation of the New Testament to the Christian tradition subsequent to it and, in various ways and degrees, dependent upon it. Putting it more sharply, it is also the question of the relation of such studies to the Church. Historically, that relation has in this respect served New Testament scholarship well, despite all that may be put on the debit side. It is plainly a fact that if it had not been for the belief that the study of the New Testament was necessary to the Church, especially in the training of its clergy, the subject would not have the prominence which it still enjoys in many theological faculties and departments; and it is arguable that, if it should depend on justification on that ground, it no longer merits its present prominence. Largely through forswearing anachronism academically in the interests of historical realism, its own position has itself become an anachronism! But that is, once more, mere politics, a matter of pragmatic observation, and we need not necessarily feel a sense of obligation because of the history of our subject. There is the more substantial question of the relationship of New Testament studies to the Christian tradition. Leaving to the historians its purely historical aspects, how are we to understand and handle that relationship? Is there any relationship which falls to our responsibility, and if so, how are we to discharge it? Here, if anywhere, New Testament theology may surely find a place as a distinct, reputable and perhaps obligatory subject.

One possibility is that we should adopt a sweet-and-sour approach and give the historians their head – in a theological spirit. It is not a common view, but we may hold that each Christian period (including the first period of all), of course overlapping with those before and after it, has validity in its own right, and, theologically and morally, neither owes debts to its predecessors nor has authority over its successors. It simply 'happened', as a stage along the providential way. Yet it is hard to be content with that procedure as far as the New Testament period is concerned. To put the matter at its least demanding level, while the Christian religion remains in some sense a faith derived from and dependent upon Jesus and does not see itself as simply freewheeling through history, the New Testament witness to him has a privileged position – even from a purely empirical point of view and apart from theological considerations. It is possible for Chalcedon, Trent or Calvin's *Institutes* to be seen as points along the way rather than authorities in a way that the New Testament writings cannot be. However historical and relativistic the regard we bring to them, they have had and have not wholly lost a defining role in the Christian tradition – difficult though it may be to describe satisfactorily. It follows that New Testament studies will fail in so far as they do not take account of that role. No doubt they can, in their most self-contained mood, find justification in terms of the pursuit of truth and so fend off marauding vice-chancellors; but that will not remove the claim exercised by their actual place in Christian tradition and by present-day Christian theology as it looks to them, insistently yet obscurely, for help. The difficulty is to see how that claim can be met without doing violence to the integrity of historical study as it is now perceived.

It is time to attempt a positive view of the pursuit of New Testament theology in present circumstances. Certain principles may be laid down. First, no account will be satisfactory which imposes on the New Testament the later doctrinal agenda of the Church. It is historically artificial and anachronistic to undertake a study of, for example, the New Testament witness to the classical doctrine of the Trinity or of the Immaculate Conception. The shrinking of Protestant scholars (at least) from the one does not always prevent them from being attracted to the other. Neither is admissible. It is of course possible to identify elements of New Testament thought or texts within the New Testament which, as a matter of fact, played a part in the development and eventual formulation and defence of either doctine, or else, with hindsight, may be seen to adumbrate that development, but that is a different matter from 'witness'. Only a Newman-like view of the New Testament writers, seeing them as in some way, even unconsciously and indefinitely, imbued with the whole doctrinal edifice of Christianity, would justify such an approach.[12]

Second, no account will be satisfactory which treats the New Testament as having a corporate mind. Such a procedure, drawing upon all its components at will, may be possible for those of high canonical principle, but no longer can it hope to win wide acceptance; and the very fact that it must be argued for with difficulty and cannot assume a position of natural command makes a radical difference to its status. While it is legitimate to trace possible influences (though they are rarely crystal clear) from one New Testament writer to another, even to the point of suggesting trajectories of ideas which develop as they speed through early Christian space, the weight must fall on the particular minds at work in the writings and their identification.[13] Unless we are deliberately to risk a clouded view, there is no going back from the theology of Mark, Matthew or Luke to 'the theology of the synoptic Gospels' – however strong our belief in Q as a force within two of them. It may turn out that a particular writing will not yield to interpretation as the work of a single author, but must be the product of a number of not wholly compatible minds. Nevertheless, the writing as it stands, however it reached its present state, represents a certain fusion of minds which once interacted, albeit imperfectly, in a way that the canonical collection as a whole does not.[14]

A weaker form of the 'corporate New Testament mind' approach may still appear to be valid. Surely a term like 'kingdom of God' or 'Lord' or 'saviour', found in a number of different New Testament writings, has a meaning, or cluster of meanings, which makes it possible to discuss it independently of a particular writer and in a consideration of New Testament theology as a whole. Such a discussion forms a legitimate step after the elucidation of such terms in relation to the contemporary Jewish or Hellenistic background. But, as far as the New Testament is concerned, it is only a step on the way to the only plain reality before us – a series of discrete texts and contexts. However thorough our general understanding of 'kingdom of God', interpretation has to reckon with *this* writer's meaning in *this* specific setting within *his* work as a whole. The unit is not the term itself but the theological thought of the writer who uses it.[15]

Third, no approach will be satisfactory which wilfully neglects the total cultural context of either the New Testament writers or the modern interpreter. Perhaps what is required in this respect is not so much the achievement of perfection as the provision of a brake on foolishness. New Testament theology has suffered much from the attribution to theological ideas in the New Testament of a kind of timelessness and the bestowing on texts, originally transient in their significance, of eternal seriousness.[16] New Testament theology, more than any other branch of New Testament study, finds it hard to abandon the belief that, in some fairly strong sense, Scripture was written for *our* learning. Awareness of cultural context is much the most effective antidote to such belief, though it works less by countering than by bypassing it. The outcome is a sense of distance[17] between the original context and our own, which at first sight inhibits anything other than a descriptive theological account and on any showing compels doctrinal reflection which is filtered and indirect.

These principles appear to present a massive deterrent to any theological work with the New Testament that is other than analytic and descriptive. They seem to forbid any movement out from New Testament study in a doctrinal direction of a general or synthesizing character. At most, they might license a theologically vague inspirational force from the New Testament to us, a carrying-over of sentiment, exercising over us no kind of control. Yet anything lacking these features falls under the condemnation of ignoring historical realism – and the disadvantages of that are only too obvious.

Edward Schillebeeckx, in his two books *Jesus* and *Christ*,[18] adopts what is essentially a pragmatic as much as a theoretical approach. To be recognizable as well as legitimate, Christian theology must work with two interests in mind, move between two poles: on the one side, Christian origins, the pristine expressions of faith, and on the other side, the present setting within which, in all its complex appreciation of truth, faith must now operate. It is uncertain whether this is better described as the work of a New Testament theologian determined to be fully open to the present context of doctrinal statement or of a dogmatic theologian determined not to force the New Testament evidence into an historically alien mould. In effect, he stands squarely with one foot on either side of the divide; and though, from the standpoint of New Testament studies, his work lacks a certain sharpness of historical focus, at least the principle of the limited historical context of the New Testament writings is fully accepted. Such an approach is pragmatic in the sense that a Christianity which ignores its origins seems bound to lack definition and identity.

But how, in Schillebeeckx's account, are the two poles connected? Not, it appears, by attributing authoritative status to the continuous process of Christian theological development which links them at the temporal level. That would be to court incoherence and intellectual suffocation. It is Christian origins and the ever-changing Christian present which specially merit Christian theological attention; and the link is, once more partly pragmatically, to be found by way of key features which dominate the early Christian scene: the conviction of Christ as living, the awareness of 'salvation', and the sense of a new, expectant community of God's people. Those beliefs form the essential legacy of earliest Christianity, as witnessed in the New Testament, and the essential reality of any Christianity worthy of the name now or, presumably, at any time.[19]

Such a view has much to be said for it. It avoids the narrowness of some older biblical theology, with its closeness of working with biblical language and thought-forms; yet it preserves an intelligibly biblical vision. The pragmatic quality of this approach is attractive in that it helps bridge the gap between historical objectivity and particularity on the one hand and doctrinal truth on the other, which has proved such a chasm in the light of recent trends in New Testament studies. It provides a link between origins and the present while leaving the latter an undefined – perhaps because indefinable – measure of autonomy. The question of present doctrine is not to be answered solely by reference to the Christian past, even to Christian beginnings: work remains for us to do. Nevertheless, how it is to be answered remains obscure.

But the picture Schillebeeckx paints is not without hints for further progress; for it indicates certain lines of method. And the principles we laid down reinforce them. It is plain that earliest Christian theology did not spring ready-made from within the Christian movement itself. In all its forms, it represented an amalgam of elements, some drawn from the common stock of contemporary beliefs, some quite novel, resulting from the impulse of Jesus, others the unstable products of the impact of the latter upon the former, the effects of imperfect and only partly coherent reflection. But it was an amalgam which belonged to those unique circumstances.

Let me then propose, as a first contribution to doctrine from New Testament studies, viewed in the light of my principles, a sense of the relative autonomy of doctrine as a present pursuit. This is a devastating contribution indeed. Is not doctrine, by its very nature, bound to the tradition, and incapable of identity if severed from it? Its practitioners will vary in the degree of admitted or desired debt to the prevailing culture, but 'autonomy' is scarcely a word they readily allow to spring to their lips. Yet New Testament scholars, acting in their own right, now have a duty to bring it to their attention. New Testament scholars spend their lives studying the New Testament documents within their original context and quite regardless of their future destiny. They have no responsibility to see them as propelled towards Chalcedon or supporting Lutheran orthodoxy or tending towards the eucharistic teaching favoured by Vatican II Catholicism. If anything, they are likely to point to their alien quality in relation to later developments. They must, of course, acknowledge the force of tradition and the reality of continuity in belief and practice, but they cannot forbear, as they look out towards the history of the Church, to indicate the measure of illusion which invariably afflicts those who claim to be in a tradition of faith.[20] Continuity of institution there may be, change and development of belief there always are. Whether because of sheer ignorance of times past or because of the irresistible pressure of new cultural assumptions, there is always change in the proportion, the perspective and the very content of belief. New Testament scholars are used to seeing the shift from Paul to the writer of the Pastoral Epistles or even Ephesians as already seismic. There is then every propriety in pointing to the great measure of autonomy each new theological generation exercises, even if it denies it with every breath and swears allegiance to the faith once delivered.

There is then the question: now that it has come to the surface, how may doctrine use this autonomy? It is one thing to exercise it unconsciously, the conscious mind being filled with thoughts of faithfulness to the past, quite another to feel the responsibility of exercising autonomy, within an undoubted continuity of life and witness. Is it a matter of defining in advance limits of adaptation, drawing up formulas for the legitimate translation of old beliefs into new forms, or finding criteria for distinguishing between essential and expendable, permanent and transient doctrines? New Testament theology has not lacked exponents of all these arts;[21] and often they have used them with a regrettable lack of candour or explicitness. Yet all suffer from superficiality and a lack of that historical realism whose demands can no longer be refused.

The recognition of such autonomy, as an inevitable condition of life, may fill the theologian with alarm. But his nerve may be restored by a second contribution from New Testament scholarship as it turns in the direction of the doctrinal task. Once more, it does not, initially, go beyond the bounds of factual observation. It consists of an analysis of the procedure by which earliest Christian faith arose. It is, be it noted, for this purpose a matter of procedure rather than of content. The New Testament scholar can offer a sight of that procedure at a stage in Christian history marked by relative simplicity, before the complexities arising from faithfulness to a developing tradition existed. Without in the least subscribing to myths of a golden age, we can say that it shows, from a conceptual point of view, a kind of pristine purity.

It is an over-simplification, yet far from being a falsehood or a gross distortion, to say that the Christian faith began with the impact of the career of Jesus (whether perceived as a whole or in terms of some part of it). It is an over-simplification because only the gnostic or Marcionite Jesus appears like a bolt from the non-historical blue. Of course we are concerned with his cultural and social antecedents and keen to understand him in the light of them. But no amount of such understanding succeeds in making him merge wholly into his background.[22] Nor is it simply the weight of later and possibly misguided faith which prevents his disappearance from the foreground. It is a matter of his immediate historical impact. It may be that his role was speedily inflated beyond all reason – that is a matter for argument – but the fact of substantial immediate impact, unrivalled among Jewish contemporaries who can be put forward for comparison, is undeniable.

Yet what is available to us as wholly incontrovertible and objective is (we must, however reluctantly, admit) only the *fact* of his impact. The very moment it is observable to us, from the response of those who felt and received it, subjectivity and diversity arose. We cannot penetrate behind the social, cultural and personal particularity of those receivers of Jesus. Of course, they are not in reality so diverse in their particularity that no intelligible picture can emerge and no statement, of greater or lesser probability, concerning the Jesus whose impact they experienced, can be made. But in principle, particularity, the contribution of the one who receives, enters in and can never again be banished.

It enters initially in the form of experience. This experience too is, strictly, hidden from us; in the purely factual sense that, with the possible and in any case highly problematic exception of Paul, we have no access to those who received the power of Jesus in the flesh; also in the sense that experience, in this sense, is inarticulate, inward, even powerful by virtue of its word-transcending quality. Nevertheless, it can, however hesitantly, be surmised and characterized.[23] It is not of first importance for our purpose that we describe it accurately, only that we identify the *fact* of it: there *was* such subjectively conditioned experience. We may call it, to use the most general terms, an experience of salvation, of new well-being in relation to God. Its precise nature would naturally depend on the pre-existing need and disposition of those concerned. What is more, it would be wholly limited by that need and disposition. It may be in a particular case that only the arousing of the experience of salvation really brought to awareness a sense of need: did Paul see the Law as inadequate except in the light of Christ?[24] Even so the principle holds: a man experiences salvation, however self-transcending it may enable him to be, only in terms of his own existing equipment of mind and personality. It was not open to Paul to feel the impact of Christ in terms of *nirvana* or an assurance of a future preferential migration of his soul, but only in some relation to the Law which dominated the horizon of his dealings with God.

Such experience is visible to us only through its having received verbal, indeed written, expression. That move brings further obliqueness.[25] While it makes communication and permanence possible, it also brings new limitation. It is true that, under the force of profound experience, old words may be pressed into new work;[26] but still, if a writer is to be intelligible, he must use the stock of words available to him. More precisely than at the stage of experience, he is the creature of his setting: the creature and, from the point of view of later times and of contemporaries who are significantly different from him, tragically even the victim. Written expression is both a blessing and a curse. It leads to the sharing of experience, but also to its being objectified. Indeed, if the written words then go on to acquire formal authority, with the agreement of others who have not known the initial experience, they acquire, in relation to that experience, a distorting and a distancing role. They may command assent and inspire new experience, but they are heard with new ears and repeated by new lips. Church formulations are bound to have this character: negotiation and consensus mean a loss of immediacy to particular experience.

Blessing or curse, the process thus outlined is that by which Christian theology set off on its journey. It is a process constantly repeated ever since, whatever modifications and whatever increase in complexity are brought by the passage of time; especially as new expressions of faith create new experience and encapsulate the whole process in themselves. Each new repetition brings its own shifts, its own new injection of the particular, however unwilling and unaware. Theology, as an expression of faith, is ever creative and ever unfaithful to the tradition, if faithfulness is measured by fixity. May not New Testament scholarship urge upon doctrine the franker recognition, and then the welcoming, of this inevitable character of the doctrinal process and task, with its necessary autonomy and its innovatory role? It involves naturally a quite transformed attitude to the formulas and beliefs of the past. It will not be a matter of either guiltily striving to keep dying beliefs alive by some kind of reinterpretation or discarding them as if they had always been somehow erroneous. The expression of the experience of salvation is always more or less inadequate, and yet has within its context a certain validity; but it always tends to be more confident and less provisional in its claims than its content justifies. Even in the best hands, it is only an attempt to achieve the impossible. 'Autonomy' is then a serious word. There are no exemptions from its rule, no enclaves of doctrine exempt from its effects, no items of belief which come down to a later period immune from change and somehow sacrosanct, no predetermined key beliefs which have a right to persist at all costs.

Making the most of any standing we have so far obtained, we who begin from the New Testament side have a more threatening contribution to offer to those whose business is the elucidation and statement of doctrine (and indeed to ourselves when we extend towards that task). Our chief professional glory is our sensitivity to history, our feeling for the New Testament circumstances in themselves, with their variety and their strangeness. We cannot but offer that sensitivity both to those whose concern with other and wider periods or aspects of Christian life has not so far led them, as a group and a discipline, to share its keenness and to those whose interest is primarily not historical but the present statement of Christian doctrine. For the former, it is only a matter of time. It is unlikely that there will be any more reputable histories of Christian doctrine which neglect the social and cultural circumstances in which doctrine has come to birth.[27] Accounts of Christian belief which give an impression of disembodied timelessness or of the pure interiority of beliefs will cease to be acceptable. It is a process which can surely now be left to take its course. But it is less predictable that, without encouragement, those whose concern is the present statement of Christian doctrine will acquire reflective sensitivity to their own social and cultural formation and to its effect upon the doctrine they think and write.[28]

Suppose they are freed somewhat by recognition of the necessary relative autonomy of each period (indeed, each thinker and writer) in the interaction of experience and its formal expression; then it is a still harder step to state doctrine for oneself with a full sense of its transience and its deeply conditioned quality. Indeed, the recognition of such limitation may occasion the collapse of the enterprise or at the very least the muting of its confidence as doctrinal statement; and what is the good of Christian doctrine unless it is kerygmatic in tone and style? Not to go beyond elucidation is to run the risk of death. So the contribution of New Testament scholarship may turn out to be the demise of doctrine as a pursuit, at any rate as traditionally understood. All, it may seem at first sight, because of insistence on certain fundamental and pervasive points about method. New Testament scholarship presents the methods it has come to adopt, and simply claims that they are equally and necessarily applicable to matters of doctrine. Only an academic timelag has prevented their use with comparable rigour in other spheres of theological study.

But to leave the matter at the level of method is to underestimate the seriousness of the contribution New Testament studies have to make to doctrine. It is also a matter of content. The historical sensitivity which New Testament scholars have so long cultivated leads to the realization that Christian belief changes from one period to another, not simply in emphasis, not by steady unfolding or more careful definition, but in shape and content, as one cultural environment gives place to another. Patterns of belief that centred on the coming end of all things were not simply adjusted, they died away. That crucial factor simply lost its dynamic and pervasive role. The centuries-long preoccupation of practical Christian belief with death, not only as the focus of piety but also as the matter in relation to whch salvation and morals were inescapably considered, has become for very many Christians, including those who write doctrine, a thing of the past, no longer capable of playing its determinative part.[29] These shifts are as significant as any that can be imagined. They have not been the result of conscious reflection in the Christian community at either the popular or the official level; on neither question has any change of teaching been promulgated. Yet it is hard to think of any matters in relation to which such shift of belief is more profound in its effects on the whole Christian doctrinal identity.

The effect is to give to doctrine in any period a more constructive role and a greater responsibility, and at the same time a more experimental tone. It can have no expectation of finality, just as it cannot reckon merely to restate the inherited beliefs of the past. It cannot see itself as momentous, and can feel a certain freedom in reacting to the circumstances of the time. At the same time, its scope may be dramatically reduced and simplified.

Sheerly at the factual level, Christian theology, to be recognizable, must attend to its beginnings in relation to Jesus. We outlined the pattern of those beginnings from a theological point of view. It was a matter of response to Jesus and of the expression of experience to which he gave rise. Making allowance for the stangeness, to us, of the thought-forms and terminology used, we may feel a certain simplicity in that process. It was a far cry from the structure of distinct but interlocking beliefs that later came to constitute Christian doctrine. There was, in essence, just a range of ways of responding to Jesus as the decisive agent of God, or, to put it more formally but already perhaps too woodenly, a range of christologies within the setting of a range of eschatological patterns and images. In the terms of later formal doctrine, and so anachronistically, Christology, soteriology and eschatology filled the picture. The rest of so-called doctrine was really the application or extension to other matters of this central conviction about Jesus. Even to refer to the New Testament faith as 'doctrine' is to risk importing formal and structural considerations that are wholly alien to the situation.

In that sense, the message of New Testament studies to doctrine is a counsel of simplicity and the warning that much of alleged doctrinal debate may be factitious and misconceived. In the light of the concerns of the New Testament and its conception of what constitutes Christian belief, what intelligible basis can there be for the controversies about the sacraments or the ministry or the nature of the Church which have long been so high on the doctrinal agenda? The sense in which these matters are 'theological' can only be in relation to the question: what are the implications of the mission of Jesus, and the understanding of God derived from him, for these matters in the context of the present life of his followers? There is no 'timeless revelation' on these matters for us to receive and use.

It has become fashionable to emphasize the story of Jesus as the centre of the power of the Christian message, as distinct from concepts and doctrines. In so far as it is suggested that attention to the story was the way of the first Christians, then plainly it is far from being the whole truth. The first Christian writer, Paul, may indeed have held to the story, but it was, for all we can tell, in its barest form and denuded of all narrative power. Paul was firmly a man of doctrine. Yet modern New Testament study is right to emphasize the power of the story of Jesus for many early Christians.[30] It was what they were presented with and nourished by. The story of Jesus, or rather, we have to say once more, the stories of Jesus – for we cannot penetrate behind the variety of ways in which his story was told and he was regarded. Yet, despite the variety, there is unity in the *fact* of the story, so that Christian theology then had this fertile, imaginative quality, this inescapable potentiality for growth and movement. Much of that potentiality was stunted or wasted as conceptuality, doctrine, came to predominate in the Hellenic church; some of it ran to seed in gnostic myth-making. Still, attentiveness to the story is a permanent offering from the New Testament to the Church and from New Testament scholarship to doctrine. It has the importance of indicating that doctrine should not, if undertaken in its traditional ways and according to its conventional understanding of itself, rule the roost in Christian endeavour but take its place within the rich variety constituted by prayer, liturgy, ethics and common Christian life. In all these spheres, the story of Jesus will continue to exercise its non-directive, open power, ready to give rise to new and unforeseeable effects. New Testament theology's happiest and central task may be simply to present the story as honestly and vividly as it can, hoping that Christians will absorb the lessons of its mode as well as its content.

In sum, New Testament studies have the opportunity to set the doctrinal enterprise in a new light and to invite a reassessment of its nature. The result may at first sight be felt to be a reduction in the scope and importance of that enterprise. Certainly, it may more easily, yet surely advantageously, merge with other kinds of Christian discourse: apologetics, ethics, spirituality. The fluidity and even anarchy we noted at the start may be increased, but the hope is that this will be in the interests of the accessibility of the gospel.[31]

NOTES

1 For an account of New Testament theology as a subject, see 'New Testament Theology' by John Ziesler in Alan Richardson and John Bowden (eds), *A New Dictionary of Christian Theology*, London 1983; R. Morgan, *The Nature of New Testament Theology*, London 1973; W. G. Kümmel, *The New Testament: the History of the Investigation of its Problems*, London 1973; L. Goppelt, *Theology of the New Testament* I (Grand Rapids 1981), pp. 251–81.

2 For example, R. Bultmann's *Theology of the New Testament*, London 1952, takes a historical and descriptive path but is imbued with firm doctrinal purpose of a Lutheran-existentialist kind.

3 Such a programme determines the analysis given in H. Ridderbos, *Paul, an Outline of his Theology*, London 1975, but starting from a New Testament point of view. For an example of a dogmatic theologian turning to the New Testament for texts and topics, it is instructive to reflect on the procedure in a work like J. Macquarrie, *Principles of Christian Theology*, London 1966; for instance, the treatment of angels, pp. 215–18.

4 Thus, doctrinal positions and credal assertions about the Holy Spirit were arrived at in the fourth century on the basis of New Testament texts (for example, 'Lord' in the Nicene Creed, cf. 2 Corinthians 3.17), whose original sense is now seen to be quite other, as they are viewed within their first-century setting and in the context of the thought of the particular New Testament writer. (See J. N. D. Kelly, *Early Christian Creeds* (London 1950), pp. 338ff.)

5 As in the case of a writer like Hegel whose starting-point is a frankly philosophical framework.

6 For example, the work of Maurice Wiles (especially *Faith and the Mystery of God*, London 1982, and the earlier *What is Theology?*, London 1976) and Schubert Ogden (for example, *The Point of Christology*, London 1982).

7 Such as: why attend to this first-century literature anyway? Why attach importance to Jesus' self-understanding or opinions?

8 This has been a major factor in the demise of the biblical theology

fashionable a generation ago, see 'Biblical Theology' by J. L. Houlden in Alan Richardson and John Bowden (eds), *A New Dictionary of Christian Theology*, London 1983; James Barr, *The Bible in the Modern World*, London 1973: ibid., *Explorations in Theology* 7, London 1980.

9 Often seen as a weakness, brought to the surface by increased historical sensitivity, in the work of R. Bultmann; see especially *Jesus Christ and Mythology*, London 1960.

10 From the Platonism of the patristic period onwards.

11 Recent structuralist studies of parts of the New Testament are in mind (for example, essays in Xavier Léon-Dufour, *Les Miracles de Jésus selon le Nouveau Testament*, Paris 1977), of which a carefully modifed example, by John Drury, is included in this volume. In another mode, see also the work of Northrop Frye, for example, *The Great Code*, London 1982, treating the Bible as a literary whole.

12 See C. E. Gunton, *Yesterday and Today*, London 1983, for an optimistic view (which many New Testament scholars would not share) of the essential presence of classical Christology in the New Testament or at any rate of the high degree of continuity between the two.

13 See J. L. Houlden, *Ethics and the New Testament*, London 1973, ch. 1.

14 This paragraph is an assertive statement representing a whole world of modern New Testament scholarship: see J. Rohde, *Rediscovering the Teaching of the Evangelists*, London 1968; E. Best, *Mark, the Gospel as Story*, Edinburgh 1983; W. Kelber, *The Oral and the Written Gospel*, Philadelphia 1983; J. D. G. Dunn, *Unity and Diversity in the New Testament*, London 1977.

15 For an example of a thorough and balanced approach to this aspect, see B. Lindars, *Jesus Son of Man*, London 1983.

16 For a discussion of this question, see the work of D. E. Nineham, especially *The Use and Abuse of the Bible*, London 1976, and *Explorations in Theology 1*, London 1977.

17 The powerful message of Albert Schweitzer in *The Quest of the Historical Jesus*, London 1910.

18 Schillebeeckx's approach is described chiefly in parts one and four of *Christ*, London 1980, and in his *Interim Report on the Books Jesus and Christ*, London 1980.

19 Readers may like to compare S. W. Sykes, *The Identity of Christianity*, London 1984, part three.

20 See Robert Wilken, *The Myth of Christian Beginnings*, London 1979.

21 Contrast the relegation to secondary status by Luther of the Epistle of James, judged by the test of justification by faith; or the contrast between the inferior position given to the Pastoral Epistles by E. Käsemann and others (because of their witness to 'early catholicism') and the weight put upon them by many Anglican theologians (because of their alleged witness to catholic church order).

22 Contrast essays five and six (by A. E. Harvey and G. Vermes) in A. E.

Harvey (ed.), *God Incarnate, Story and Belief*, London 1981, for their accounts of the historical role of Jesus as a basis for faith in him.

23 See John Knox, *The Death of Christ*, London 1959, part three.

24 See E. P. Sanders, *Paul and Palestinian Judaism*, London 1977; ibid. *Paul, the Law and the Jewish People*, Philadelphia 1983; H. Räisänen, *Paul and the Law*, Tübingen 1983.

25 See W. Kelber, *The Oral and the Written Gospel*, Philadelphia 1983; E. D. Hirsch, *The Aims of Interpretation*, Chicago 1976.

26 See David Hill, *Greek Words and Hebrew Meanings*, Cambridge 1967.

27 It is instructive to contrast a standard 'plain' history of doctrine such as J. N. D. Kelly, *Early Christian Doctrines*, London 1958, with the understanding of the same period derived from works such as Peter Brown, *Augustine of Hippo*, London 1967, and R. A. Markus, *Christianity in the Roman World*, London 1974. See also J. H. S. Kent, *The End of the Line?* London 1983.

28 'Less predictable': note the pressures on a body like the Church of England's Doctrine Commission in recent years to move from questions of method and the setting of doctrine to questions of content – what is to be believed. It is reflected in the contrast between the two publications, *Christian Believing*, London, and *Believing in the Church*, London, issued in 1976 and 1981.

29 See J. McManners, *Death and the Enlightenment*, Oxford 1981; G. Rowell, *Hell and the Victorians*, Oxford 1974.

30 See E. Best, *Mark, the Gospel as Story*, Edinburgh 1983; A. E. Harvey (ed.), *God Incarnate, Story and Belief*, London 1981.

31 This essay was delivered as a paper at the conference of the British section of the Society for New Testament Studies held in Edinburgh in September 1984.

Index